ECONOMICS AND ELECTIONS

"Vote-buying starts early." Mr. Nigel Lawson, Chancellor of the Exchequer (KAL, *The Economist,* Nov. 22, 1985, 57)

ECONOMICS AND ELECTIONS

The Major Western Democracies

Michael S. Lewis-Beck

Ann Arbor
The University of Michigan Press

First paperback edition 1990
Copyright © by The University of Michigan 1988
All rights reserved
Published in the United States of America by
The University of Michigan Press
Manufactured in the United States of America

1991   1990   4   3   2

Library of Congress Cataloging-in-Publication Data

Lewis-Beck, Michael S.
    Economics and elections : the major western democracies / Michael
S. Lewis-Beck.
        p.   cm.
    Bibliography: p.
    Includes index.
    ISBN 0-472-10099-8 (alk. paper). — ISBN 0-472-08133-0 (pbk.: alk. paper)
    1. Voting—Europe.   2. Voting—United States.   3. Elections—
Europe.   4. Elections—United States.   5. Europe—Economic
conditions—1945– —Public opinion.   6. United States—Economic
conditions—1945– —Public opinion.   7. Public opinion—Europe.
8. Public opinion—United States.   I. Title.
JN94.A956L48 1988
324.9′055—dc19   88-26183
                                                              CIP

Preface

How does economics influence elections in the leading Western democracies? In various ways, this book tells the story of that connection. The raw materials are national election surveys and time series observations from Britain, France, Germany, Italy, Spain, and the United States. These data, as analyzed by myself and others, serve to develop economic voting models for these countries. In the composition of this statistical essay, I was filled with intellectual excitement and a sense of adventure. It gave me the opportunity to answer interesting, even worthy, questions about the relationship of politics and economics.

Here are some general ones. Does a government's fate at the ballot box hinge on the state of the economy? Is it inflation, unemployment, or income that makes the difference? What triggers economic voting for or against the incumbent? That is, do voters look at their pocketbook, or the national accounts? Are their judgments based on past economic performance, or future policy promises? Are such evaluations "reasoned" calculations, or "emotional" reactions? Do economic voters "punish" rulers for bad times, but fail to "reward" them for good times? How well can economic fluctuations predict election results? If economics has such a strong impact on individual voters, then why is there no political business cycle?

Many of the questions are aimed at Western European voting behavior, a special focus of this study. How important is an economic explanation of the Western European vote choice, when compared to more traditional explanations, such as social class, religion, or partisan ideology? Is the same structural model of economic voting applicable across Western European nations? What accounts for the differences in strength of economic voting that do exist? In these European electorates, does economics represent just another campaign issue that, like other issues, comes and goes? More generally, how should economic issues be featured in Western European voting models?

The list of questions is stimulating. In the chapters that follow, I propose answers to them, and others. I do not expect the reader to accept, without quarrel, each finding and conclusion. (After all, controversy lies at the heart of this literature!) Nevertheless, I hope that the reader will derive satisfaction from the unfolding of the investigation itself and, perhaps, decide at the end that economics really does have a lot to do with elections.

Acknowledgments

I have many individuals to thank for help on this project. First comes the network of individuals connected to the Euro-Barometer. Jacques-René Rabier, founder and director (until 1987) of these European Community surveys, gave encouragement and advice all along the way. Ron Inglehart (University of Michigan), co-director with Mr. Rabier, facilitated the transatlantic organization of the research, as well as providing intellectual and moral support. Hélène Riffault, director of *Faits et Opinion,* which oversaw the actual surveys, afforded an abundance of practical guidance on the field operations. These individuals worked closely with me in preparing the economic questions included in Euro-Barometers Nos. 20 and 21 (1983 and 1984). In addition, others provided useful suggestions on item construction, namely Stanley Feldman (University of Kentucky), Douglas Hibbs (University of Göteborg), Kai Hildebrandt (University of Windsor), and Rod Kiewiet (California Institute of Technology).

Besides the Euro-Barometers, a special battery of questions was prepared for the Michigan Surveys of Consumer Attitudes (1984), thereby introducing political questions into these otherwise exclusively economic surveys. Richard Curtin and his staff, at the Monitoring Economic Changes Program (Institute for Social Research), were professional and cooperative. With regard to tips on construction of the American items, I would like particularly to acknowledge Don Kinder (University of Michigan).

This enterprise has also benefited, directly or indirectly, from discussions and collaborations with various students of political economy. In addition to those already mentioned, I refer especially to Elias M. Amor Bravo (University of Valencia), Paolo Bellucci (University of Campobasso), Jean-Dominique Lafay (University of Paris I), Helmut Norpoth (State University of New York at Stony Brook), Martin Paldam (University of Aarhus), and Jean-Jacques Rosa (Institut d'Etudes Politiques). Beyond the economic voting sphere, this work has profited from conversations with an active group of scholars of Western European mass behavior, including Ron Inglehart and Sam Barnes (University of Michigan), Russ Dalton (Florida State University), and Bing Powell (University of Rochester). Finally, I must recognize my occasional co-authors on the subject, from whom I have learned a great deal: Paolo Bellucci, Heinz

Eulau (Stanford University), Tom Lancaster (Emory University), and Tom Rice (University of Vermont).

Of course, the research would not have been possible without organizational support. The United States National Science Foundation awarded the grant (No. SES 83-06020) that funded the questionnaire items in the Euro-Barometers and the Consumer Surveys. The German Marshall Fund appointed me a Senior Research Fellow, which allowed time to write. The University of Iowa helped in many ways, providing me a sabbatical leave, a supportive research environment, and a bright group of political science graduate assistants, including Tom Holbrook-Provow, Steve Nelson, Andy Skalaban, and Blake Wood. Of course, none of these individuals or organizations is responsible for any interpretations or errors the text contains.

Some of the book material was considered earlier in articles I authored (or coauthored), the following in particular: "Economic conditions and executive popularity: The French experience," *American Journal of Political Science* 24 (1980): 306–23; "Pocketbook voting in U.S. national election studies: Fact or artifact?," *American Journal of Political Science* 29 (1985): 348–56; "Comparative economic voting: Britain, France, Germany, Italy," *American Journal of Political Science* 30 (1986): 315–46; "Economic influences on legislative elections in multiparty systems: France and Italy," with Paolo Bellucci, *Political Behavior* 4 (1982): 93–107; "Economics and the American voter: Past, present, future," *Political Behavior* 10 (1988): 5–21. I thank these journals for the necessary permissions to draw from these articles. Also, *The Economist* is to be thanked for permission to reproduce the caricature of Nigel Lawson, by KAL, in the November 22, 1985, issue, p. 57.

Contents

Figures

Tables

Part 1 Context and Theory

How Economics Defeated Iowa Statehood:
A Historic Example

By the 1830s, the Territory of Iowa was rapidly being settled. Governor Lucas thought the time was right for statehood and pressed the legislative assembly to put the question to the people. The assembly yielded and, on the August, 1840, election ballot, asked whether a state constitutional convention should be called. The voters overwhelmingly rejected this statehood proposal, with 2,907 against and 937 for.

Why did the territorial citizenry not aspire to more lofty political status? Economics. Writing to a friend in December, 1839, a farmer named John Brown articulated the financial case against becoming a state:

> While Iowa remains a Territory, the Genl. Government pays all the Territorial expenses, which I consider a matter of much importance to the people at present, as they have no land taxable yet nor will have soon . . . consequently you will have nothing but personal property to tax . . . . And furthermore, while it remains a Territory, Congress will make appropriations for improvement of the roads and rivers. (*Annals of Iowa*, 3d ser., 8 (1907): 147)

In a subsequent vote, the people of the territory once more defeated the governor's motion for a constitutional convention. However, in April, 1844, the issue was again placed on the ballot and, by a considerable margin, the electorate decided in favor. Therefore, in October, 1844, the convention gathered at Iowa City to write the constitution for a new state.

Why did voters of the Iowa Territory suddenly change their minds and accept the mantle of statehood? Economics. The old argument on finances had been undone by the Distribution Act, passed by Congress in 1841. This act distributed money from the sale of public lands, but it could only go to states. Iowans supporting statehood contended that the funds should not be foregone since, among other things, they would cover the costs of implementing a state government. In sum, collective economic expectations again swung the voters of the Iowa Territory decisively, although this time in the opposite direction. (For a good account of this period in the history of Iowa, see Wall 1978, 38–41).

Chapter 1

Economic Problems and the Electoral Process: An Introduction

I don't think the President understands why there's high inflation and high unemployment at the same time. But then neither does anybody else. (U.S. Treasury official in Levy 1981, 50)

In the industrial democracies of the West, the post–World War II hopes of economic prosperity gave way to concerns over economic problems around 1970. Look at the United States, the leader. During the decade of the 1960s, the National Bureau of Economic Research registered no period of recession after 1961. In the subsequent ten years, however, they recorded the recessions of 1970–71, 1974–75, and yet another beginning in 1980. Further, these fluctuations had characteristics different from the usual boom-and-bust pattern. Perhaps they signaled a coming crash as we rode the latest fifty-year Kondratieff cycle, due to reach bottom as we end the 1980s. Certainly, they suggested that the traditional Phillips curve, with its trade-off of unemployment and inflation, was breaking down. Instead, a situation of stagflation reigned, with high inflation and high unemployment (or low growth) in persistent coexistence. For instance, in the United States in 1980, the inflation rate (change in the CPI) equaled 14 percent, the unemployment rate equaled 7 percent. This pattern was also observed in Western Europe (OECD figures). Here are some examples from the other five major democracies under study, for the same year, 1980: Britain, inflation equaled 18 percent, unemployment, 7 percent; France, inflation equaled 14 percent, unemployment, 6 percent; West Germany, inflation equaled 6 percent, unemployment, 3 percent; Italy, inflation equaled 21 percent, unemployment, 7 percent; Spain, inflation equaled 15 percent, unemployment, 12 percent.

Such figures led to gloomy headlines, such as this from the *Wall Street Journal* (December 2, 1982, 46): "Europe Is Adjusting to a Long Recession That Some Economists See as 'Permanent.'" A more systematic look at the changes in key macroeconomic indicators over time strengthened this pessimism. In figure 1.1 are plotted the annual unemployment rates for these six nations, since the Organization for Economic Cooperation and Development (OECD) began keeping a tally in the late 1950s. For each country, the differ-

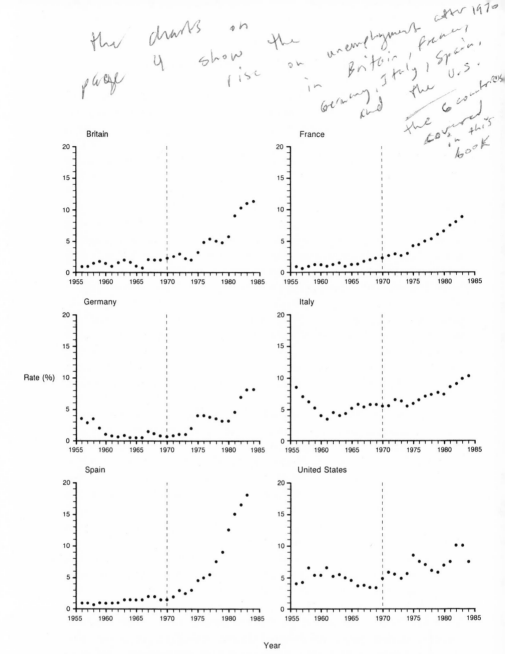

Fig. 1.1. Annual unemployment rates in the six nations. (Data from *Labor Force Statistics*, OECD.)

ence in the pre-1970 and post-1970 pattern is striking. Before 1970, the rate of unemployment is generally low, fluctuating within a narrow range. After 1970, however, unemployment begins an upward trajectory only occasionally punctuated by decline. Britain most clearly illustrates the design. From 1956 to 1969, that nation had an average unemployment rate of 1.5 percent, fluctuating only within a range of 0.9 percent to 2.0 percent. In contrast, from 1970 to 1984, its unemployment rate averaged 5.5 percent, climbing from a low of 2.1 percent in 1974 to a high of 11.2 percent in 1984.

Of course, rising unemployment rates were just a part of the economic puzzle. In evaluating trends in the economic well-being of the whole nation, it may be more useful to examine a measure of national output. In figure 1.2, therefore, are plotted the annual growth rates of the inflation-adjusted gross domestic product (GDP) in these six nations. Again, at least for most of them, 1970 appears as a dividing line. Before then, many years of healthy economic growth were experienced; but after, slow growth tended to be the rule. For some, the pattern of slow growth even seemed to be accelerating. France is the outstanding example here. In the 1960s, the annual rate of economic growth in that country was 5 to 7 percent. However, after 1970, the rate had fallen more or less steadily from that high plateau, to years of no growth, as figure 1.2 shows.

The 1980s continued to manifest high unemployment. However, growth was not quite so sluggish, and inflation certainly cooled. Here are estimates for 1987 on annual rates of unemployment, inflation, and GDP growth, respectively: Britain, 10.9, 3.5, 4.3; France, 10.6, 2.4, 2.5; Germany, 8.9, 1.0, 2.3; Italy, 14.8, 4.9, 2.4; Spain, 20.4, 4.3, 2.1; United States, 6.6, 3.9, 4.0 (*Economist*, April 23, 1988, 109). Besides these traditional macroeconomic concerns, the nations face, in varying degree, other serious economic problems, e.g., regional economic imbalance, "underground economies," gross trade deficits, and an ever-growing public sector.

The foregoing compilation of economic facts highlights the difficult policy choices that politicians of these governments have faced since the dawn of the 1970s. Interestingly, different governments have chosen different paths to economic improvement. Stagflation forced a reevaluation of the usual Keynesian fiscal tools, but left unclear the proper course to be followed. However, distinct policy alternatives unfolded from three pivotal elections: Margaret Thatcher to British prime minister in 1979, Ronald Reagan to United States president in 1980, and François Mitterrand to French president in 1981. Thatcher broke with a standard Keynesian approach, instead emphasizing a monetarist solution to the country's economic woes. Reagan touted supply-side economics, which promised less inflation, less unemployment, and less government, all in one package. Mitterrand followed socialist doctrines of nationalization and redistribution, in the context of an austerity policy of

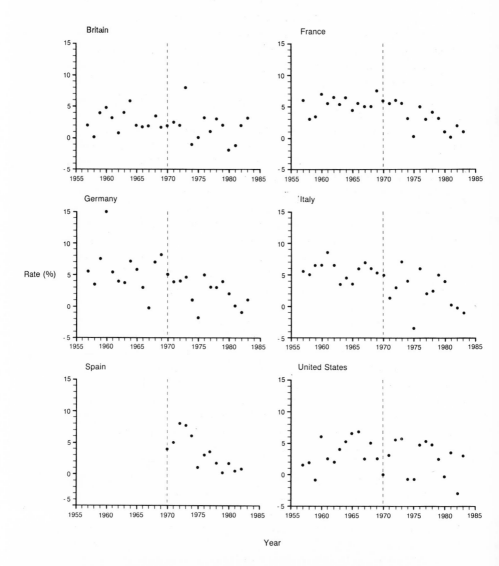

Fig. 1.2. Annual real gross domestic product (GDP) growth rate for the six nations. (Data from *National Account Aggregates,* Statistical Office of the European Communities.)

inflation adjusted annual GDP in the 6 countries

↳ slow growth dominated all of these countries except France which witnessed nearly no growth

"rigueur." *Thus, across these nations, very different policies were pursued, at roughly the same time, to solve a similar set of economic problems.*

These policies appear vindicated, in the sense that the different publics reelected all three leaders (Thatcher in 1983 and 1987, Reagan in 1984, Mitterrand in 1988). Of course, by the time of these reelections, the original policy blueprints had much changed. Nevertheless, the three still represent differences in national economic policy, differences that must be attributed, in part, to electoral fortune and cultural variation. But they also reflect, at least in their inception, honest disagreement among economic policymakers over the preferred plan of action.

Such policy disagreement is well documented in a fascinating investigation by Bruno Frey and his colleagues (1984). They surveyed over 1,500 professional economists in Belgium, France, Germany, Switzerland, and the United States, seeking their views on an array of economic policy propositions. Not unexpectedly, a good deal of consensus was found. Nevertheless, there was also considerable dissent, both within and across nations. For example, in response to the proposition, "Inflation is primarily a monetary phenomenon," United States economists divided 27 percent "yes," 30 percent "yes but," and 43 percent "no," indicating noteworthy internal disagreement over this monetarist principle. Contrast these results to those from France and Germany, two other nations in the study at hand. Germany is comparable to the United States, with 44 percent saying "no." But, for France, fully 70 percent of the sample answered "no," thereby placing it quite apart. Such differences are observed among responses to other propositions in the survey. Here are some.

Proposition: "Wage-price controls should be used to control inflation."
Responses: United States, 72 percent "no"; Germany, 93 percent "no"; France, 44 percent "no."

Proposition: "Tariffs and import quotas reduce general economic welfare."
Responses: United States, 81 percent "yes"; Germany, 70 percent "yes"; France, 27 percent "yes."

Proposition: "A minimum wage increases unemployment among young and unskilled workers."
Responses: United States, 68 percent "yes"; Germany, 45 percent "yes"; France, 17 percent "yes."

The foregoing discussion has aimed to focus attention on the serious economic problems that began in these Western nations in the 1970s and continued through the 1980s. While the problems may stand out, the solutions do not. Practicing politicians across these countries still fail to share a common plan or vision, and success remains evanescent (witness the extraordinary unemployment rates, now accepted as more or less normal). Further, trained economists disagree sharply over the proper course of action. *Surely, the average voter cannot be expected to answer policy questions that stump our political and intellectual leaders. But they can be expected to react with their ballots to how this leadership, in the end, helps or hinders the economy.*

Macroeconomic Problems and National Election Outcomes: A Preliminary Look

How do economic problems influence elections? Does a rising inflation rate cause the citizenry to "throw the rascals" out? Can declining unemployment help the government in a reelection bid? How many additional votes does accelerated economic growth bring to the incumbent? Do the economically distressed punish their legislators at the ballot box? These are intriguing and complex issues. Before plunging into these questions, I would like to present some encouraging initial impressions. The economic voting hypothesis, in its most raw form, argues that "as the economy worsens, the government losses votes." Do the simple gross fluctuations in macroeconomic conditions and election outcomes lend support to this contention? It is perhaps useful to take a look at these basic relationships, prior to entering the thicket of fully specified voting models.

By way of illustration, it is convenient first to explore the British case. Figure 1.3 plots the national percentage of the popular vote the government party received in a particular parliamentary election (on the y-axis) against a key macroeconomic indicator, the inflation rate during that year (on the x-axis), for the elections from 1959 to 1983. For example, in 1959 the ruling Conservatives received 49.4 percent of the popular vote, and the annual inflation rate was 1.0 percent. In contrast, the Labour government garnered only 36.9 percent of the vote in 1979, which had an inflation rate of 13.4 percent. The overall visual assessment of the relationship between the two variables is arresting. High rates of inflation consistently accompany low vote shares for the party in government, whether Labour or Conservative (see the lower right-hand quadrant of fig. 1.3).

This relationship appears highly predictable, with the observations closely tracking the sketched-in downward sloping line. The strong linearity suggested in this picture is confirmed by the high correlation coefficient, $r = .87$. Clearly, in contemporary Britain, it seems like a party's electoral fortune depends heavily on the performance of the economy. (Indeed, economic decline may even undo whole parties; on such causal connections, see Alt

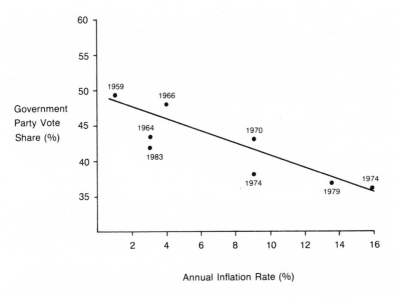

60
55
50
Government
Party Vote
Share (%)   45
40
35

Fig. 1.3. Annual inflation rate and government vote share, British general elections, 1959–83. (Data from *Labor Force Statistics*, OECD.)

1979). The June, 1987, third-term victory of Thatcher and the Conservatives suggests that the relationship continues to hold, for under her leadership the inflation rate had fallen to about 3.5 percent.

What about the relationship of economic conditions to election results in more complicated multiparty systems, where the government is seldom, if ever, composed of a single party? For example, how might economic voting construe itself in France? Notice that when an economically disgruntled citizen votes against an incumbent party, he or she is necessarily voting for the opposition. In France, across the course of the Fifth Republic (until 1981), the opposition consisted of the parties on the Left, which in fact have often joined together in formal coalition. Therefore, an expectation is that the economics-election connection could express itself in a relationship between macro-economic indicators and popular vote share for the Left opposition. In figure 1.4, one observes the scatterplot of the percentage vote in National Assembly elections (first ballot) for parties on the Left (Socialists, Communists, smaller Left parties) against the national unemployment rate, for the years 1958 to 1981. So conceived, the association is an almost perfect straight line, yielding an *r* = .93. (Only the revolutionary year of 1968 slightly spoils the geometry.) With the French case, then, raising unemployment appears to be a remarkably sure way for the government to deliver votes to the opposition. (More recent

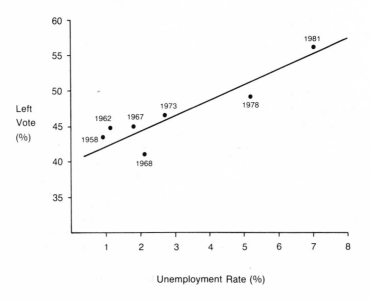

Fig. 1.4. Annual unemployment rate and vote for the Left opposition in France, National Assembly elections (first ballot), 1958–81. (Data from *Labor Force Statistics,* OECD.)

French elections also seem amenable to prediction from macroeconomic conditions; on the 1986 National Assembly contest, see Lewis-Beck 1985a, 1986a. On the 1988 presidential contest, see chap. 2.)

For Britain and France, certain standard macroeconomic indicators—the inflation rate and the unemployment rate—appear highly predictive of incumbent-opposition vote shares. Does this simple relationship hold for the other nations under study? Yes, although nowhere else are the fits as good. For the United States, a third major macroeconomic indicator, annual growth rate of real GDP, turns in a winning performance. In presidential elections (1960–84), it correlates .63 with the percentage of the popular vote going to the party currently in the White House. The suggestion that economic growth generates votes for the incumbent is repeated with the West German case. There, examining the federal elections from 1957 to 1983, real GDP growth correlated most highly with ruling party coalition vote share, $r = .51$. With regard to Italy, our fifth case, the annual inflation rate correlates more highly with election outcome than either the GDP or the unemployment variables. Looking at seven national legislative elections since 1958, the rate of inflation is found to correlate .82 with support for the Communists, the central opposition party in the Italian system.

These results are included in table 1.1, which contains the correlation of each of these three macroeconomic indicators—inflation rate, unemployment rate, GDP growth rate—with incumbent (opposition) vote share, in each country (with the exception of Spain, on which too few aggregate observations exist). Overall, these simple bivariate findings favor the argument that economic conditions shape electoral outcomes in these democracies. Every one of the correlations is in the expected direction, i.e., the worse off the economy, the worse off the incumbent. Further, most of the relationships are statistically significant at about .10 or better, despite sample sizes of only 7 or 8. (If $N = 8$, then $r > .50$ achieves significance at the .10 level, one-tail.) Also, their magnitudes are moderate to strong. Across the five countries, the average correlation of the vote variable with the inflation rate is .64, with the GDP growth rate it is .43, and with the unemployment rate it is .42.

Nevertheless, beyond a vague conclusion about aggregate bivariate patterns, the major questions remain. After more careful, multivariate work, these

TABLE 1.1   Bivariate Correlations (r) between Real GDP Growth Rate, Inflation Rate, Unemployment Rate, and Incumbent-Opposition Vote Share for Five Nations

Nation	Macroeconomic Indicator		
	GDP	Unemployment	Inflation
Britain	.16	−.20	−.87
France	−.69	.93	.60
Germany	.51	−.22	−.23
Italy	−.15	.55	.82
United States	.63	−.20	−.67

Sources: The annual macroeconomic indicators for unemployment and GDP are taken from the data sources in figures 1.1 and 1.2. The inflation figures are from the *Bulletin of Labor Statistics,* International Labor Office. The vote share variable is calculated from the following sources: C. Cook and J. Paxton, *European Political Facts 1918–1973* (New York: St. Martin's Press, 1974); J. Sallnow and A. John, *An Electoral Atlas of Europe 1968–1981* (London: Butterworth Scientific Press, 1982); *Statistical Abstract of the United States,* various issues; *Los Angeles Times,* March 7, 1983, 1. The vote variable is constructed as follows for each country: Britain, the percentage share to the government party in the general elections, 1959–83; France, the percentage for parties on the Left in the first-round balloting of National Assembly elections, 1958–81; Germany, the percentage vote to the incumbent party coalition in the federal election, 1957–83; Italy, the percentage vote to the Communist party in the national legislative elections, 1958–83; United States, the percentage of the popular presidential vote going to the party in the White House, 1956–84.

enticing implications of economic voting may come to nothing. Much serious analysis remains to be done. In the next chapter, I begin with a critique and synthesis of the aggregate time series studies, carried out by myself and many others. Then the stage is set for an in-depth analysis of economic voters in national election surveys from these six leading Western democracies.

Lewis-Beck finds that more analysis needs to be done,

therefore he begins to critique and synthesize the aggregate time series studies

Chapter 2

Macroeconomics and National Elections:
A Critique of Earlier Studies

> All political history shows that the standing of a Government and its ability to hold the confidence of the electorate at a General Election depend on the success of its economic policy. (Prime Minister Wilson, in David Watt, *Financial Times*, March 8, 1968)

> Great changes in the composition in Congress and the statehouse are due to the state of the economy. (George Gallup, October 11, 1982, *Daily Iowan*, 3A)

Earlier work on economics and elections focused on establishing links at the national level through analysis of observations gathered over time. In this regard, the pathbreaking efforts are Goodhart and Bhansali (1970), and Kramer (1971). Although by now other methodological approaches have been added, aggregate time series analysis remains an important, even exclusive, research strategy in the countries under study. These investigations merit understanding in their own right. Further, such understanding allows appreciation of the need to study individual voters in election surveys, the real research focus of this book. However, I do not intend a full review of this literature, which has already been attempted several times elsewhere (Kiewiet and Rivers 1984; Monroe 1978; Paldam 1981a; Schneider 1985). Besides, the number of relevant publications is now so vast as to defy reduction in the space of one chapter. For instance, Schneider (1985, 19) remarks that he knows of more than seventy articles on government popularity alone. Rather than take all these on, I aim to capture the flavor of the work in each country, presenting representative models, critical summaries, and a current example.[1]

While the studies have a common core, their history is slightly different from nation to nation. Whereas in some nations the matter has been pursued by examination of vote functions, in others popularity functions are the mode. In some the studies are plentiful, in others not. The discussion below takes such differences into account. I begin with Britain, giving it somewhat more attention. For not only is Britain the subject of the pivotal Goodhart and Bhansali (1970) investigation, but the efforts there are paradigmatic, capturing all the

13

strengths and weakness of the aggregate time series tradition. Next, I consider France, illustrating that the research dilemmas are not peculiar to Anglo-Saxon cases. Then, the German work, fairly plentiful but little known in the United States, is evaluated. Following that, Spain and Italy, where modeling efforts are really just beginning, are discussed. Finally comes the much-studied United States case, which I simply highlight.

After this brief country-by-country orientation, I pose a general critique of aggregate time series investigations, first, in terms of findings, and second, as a sufficient methodology for comprehending how economics moves voters in these Western democracies.

British Popularity Functions

In the winter of 1983, Prime Minister Thatcher was having trouble deciding whether to call the next general election in the summer or the autumn. Although it was not legally required until May, 1984, the prevalent assumption was that it would either be June, 1983, when the new district boundaries were in place, or October, 1983, the standard month for fall elections in Britain. The experts urged her to choose the early date. According to Alan Davies, a Barclays Bank economist, "June would give her two things: not only a low inflation rate, but the first few sparks of a recovery." Furthermore, in the words of Cambridge economist Terry Ward, "the problem with waiting until the fall is there still won't be any great recovery in her favor and inflation is likely to be going up again then" (both quotations, *Wall Street Journal*, February 4, 1983, 21). The economists, then, were making a simple argument: signs of economic improvement (here more likely to be seen in the summer) increase voter support for the government. Is such a claim, which has been echoed in the British press at least since the 1960s, justified by the evidence? Well, Thatcher called a June election, and the Conservatives won. Unfortunately, by itself, this fact has to be considered as much chance as proof. For scientific findings, we turn to the literature on popularity functions, pioneered by Goodhart and Bhansali (1970).

They seek to explain what causes "the electorate to support or to reject the government of the day" (Goodhart and Bhansali 1970, 43). Ideally, they wanted to account for the outcomes of actual elections, but the number of these was judged too few. (Apparently, this attitude continues to the present day; the only relevant study with votes as the dependent variable to have surfaced is Whiteley 1980.) Therefore, they selected for explanation the support for the government, as measured in regular national public opinion polls. Since 1947 the Gallup Poll organization has asked, on more or less a monthly basis, the following question: "If there were a General Election tomorrow, which party would you support?" The purpose to which they wish to apply this series of

[handwritten margin notes:] Thatcher called election while economy was improving and party won

responses is disarmingly straightforward. "The basic question which we asked was how far were swings in political popularity affected by economic circumstances" (Goodhart and Bhansali 1970, 45). Similarly, the methodology is unadorned. I quote it below at length, for it captures well the approach guiding the formulation of almost all popularity functions, for Britain and elsewhere:

> The basic and simple idea underlying this exercise is to take a number of variables, such as the level of unemployment, the rate of inflation, the length of time elapsed since the last election, etc., and, with the use of multiple regression analysis, to test whether variations in these selected variables have a significant effect upon political popularity as reflected in the poll figures. (Goodhart and Bhansali 1970, 44)

Here is a representative popularity function (estimated with ordinary least squares [OLS] from their analysis (Goodhart and Bhansali 1970, 62):

$$L = 12.73 - .026U_{(t-6)} - 1.25dP + .75EU - .16TR + 1.60BA$$
$$(1.86) \quad (.005) \qquad (.15) \quad (.17) \qquad (.03) \qquad (.28)$$
$$R^2 = .38 \qquad DW = .53 \qquad 246 \; df \qquad\qquad\qquad \textbf{(2.1)}$$

where L = government popularity lead (percentage declaring support for the government party minus the percentage support for the opposition party); $U_{(t-6)}$ = the number of unemployed (in thousands, seasonally adjusted), six months before; dP = the percentage change in the retail price index over the last year; EU = a postelection dummy, with the value 12 in the month after a new party victory, declining to zero across the subsequent months, and with a value of 6,6,4,2 in the four months (0 otherwise) after the incumbent party wins the election; TR = a trend dummy, with the value 1 in the first postelection month, increasing by 1 with each passing month until the next general election; BA = a back swing dummy, with values climbing from 1 to 6 in the six months (0 otherwise) before an election; the figures in parentheses are standard errors; R^2 = the coefficient of multiple determination; DW = the Durbin-Watson statistic; df = degrees of freedom (from monthly data January, 1947 to June, 1968).

In words, these results suggest that government popularity in Britain is, to a noteworthy extent, determined by two economic variables—the annual inflation rate and the unemployment level six months prior—and a set of electoral cycle variables that track the U-shaped pattern of government support (high-low-high) between elections. Moreover, after extensive further analysis (upward of sixty additional estimated equations), Goodhart and Bhansali (1970, 86) stick with this conclusion: "These two sets of factors were able to explain a large proportion of the variations in the recorded popularity of the two parties . . . . Indeed, the apparent sensitivity of political popularity to economic conditions, as shown by the equations, seems almost too much to credit.''

The case for the "political economy" hypothesis of Goodhart and Bhansali appears strong. Their arguments make common sense, and their statistical evidence supports them. Is the case closed, then? No, for subsequent research has done much to undermine the Goodhart and Bhansali work, both in general and in particular. Miller and Mackie (1973, 279), in a follow-up piece, decide that none of the economic "performance measures added much to the prediction of popularity" once the electoral cycle was taken out. Mosley (1978, 384–85), in a later study, echoes this conclusion of weak effects: "the proportions of variations in the governing party's opinion poll lead that can be explained by movements in unemployment and in the rate of change of prices alone is rather small." But in the same year, Frey and Schneider (1978, 246) disagree, arriving at "encouraging results" that show unemployment, inflation, and income to be significant influences on government popularity.

One implication, then, is that other economic variables are operating in addition to unemployment and inflation. The subsequent research of Pissarides (1980, 572) underlined this implication, for he found that percentage growth in consumption, change in the rate of inflation, percentage unemployment, and change in the dollar exchange rate all had a significant impact on popularity. Further, he strengthened the argument for the importance of the economic variables relative to the electoral cycle variables, placing "the 'typical' contribution of the electoral and economic variables at about the same level." (Pissarides 1980, 575). However, a flip-flop occurred in the next year, when Chrystal and Alt (1981a, 732) reported a popularity function in which none of the economic variables managed to achieve statistical significance. Finally, and in complete contrast, a still more recent study by Whiteley (1986) finds "that unemployment, inflation and devaluation all had a statistically significant influence on the lead of the Government."

The twists and turns in the British popularity literature must strike many observers as odd. After all, each study seeks to explain the same thing: government popularity in postwar Britain, as indicated by national polls. And each focuses on the same set of explanatory variables: macroeconomic conditions and the electoral cycle. How, then, have such wildly different conclusions been reached? The answer to this question lies in the varied research choices that were made. From study to study, the samples tend to differ in terms of size, time span, and time unit. Further, the measures are usually different, not only of the measures of economic variables but also of popularity and electoral cycle variables. And model specification, even at the conceptual level, is inconsistent from equation to equation. In addition, the timing of the electoral response (the lag structure) invariably changes. Finally, the same estimation procedures are not always followed. It is small wonder that these researchers find themselves in disagreement.

Perhaps Whiteley (1986) copes with these many difficulties as well as any. His sample is comprehensive and large, covering the period from 1947–80 (at the monthly level). With regard to measures, he taps the two most frequently used economic variables, unemployment and inflation. In addition, the model specification includes controls on the electoral cycle and economic shocks. Lastly, he resorts to Box-Jenkins transfer function estimation, which can make rejection of the null hypothesis especially difficult. Here is his general equation (Whiteley 1986, table 4, eq. 3, p. 53):

$$L_{(t)} - L_{(t-1)} = -8.45 \ln I_{(t)} - \ln I_{(t-1)} - 14.80 \ln U_{(t-8)} - .06 SHOC$$
$$\qquad\qquad\quad (2.2) \qquad\qquad\qquad (3.1) \qquad\qquad (.09)$$

$$+ \; 1.74 ELECTION - 6.13 DEVALUATION$$
$$\quad (1.15) \qquad\qquad\qquad (2.5)$$

$$+ \; .11 LABOUR + a_{(t)}[1 - .32B(1) - .20B(3)] \; \mathbf{(2.2)}$$
$$\quad (.72) \qquad\qquad\qquad (6.7) \qquad\quad (4.0)$$
$$RMS = 20.6 \qquad Chow \; stat. = 3.17$$
$$Q = 24 \qquad 24 \; df \qquad N = 406$$

where $L_{(t)} - L_{(t-1)}$ = government party lead, differenced; $\ln I_{(t)} - \ln I_{(t-1)}$ = logged annual increase in the index of retail prices, differenced; $\ln U_{(t-8)}$ = logged wholly unemployed in thousands, lagged 8 months; SHOC = dichotomous dummy variable for economic shocks, such as OPEC pricing; ELECTION = dichotomous dummy for General Election campaign; DEVALUATION = dichotomous dummy for devaluation; LABOUR = dichotomous dummy for whether Labour is in office; B = backshift operator; the figures in parentheses below the coefficients are t-ratios; RMS = mean of the residual sum of squares; Q = the Ljung-Box statistic; N = sample size.

In the face of this rigorous treatment, his unemployment and inflation measures still manage statistical significance ($|t| > 2.00$). Other popularity functions have appeared since Whiteley. While they directly take into account the effects of the Falklands war, they do not completely disconfirm the economic effects he uncovers. For instance, Norpoth (1987), in his transfer function analysis, finds that unemployment has a significant effect (although inflation does not). But Sanders, Ward, and Marsh (1987), tackling the same issues, find themselves in disagreement with Norpoth. A last word on the particulars of the controversy does not yet appear in sight. Nevertheless, something positive can be concluded: *national economic performance (variously measured) helps predict electorate support for the government in post–*

18   Economics and Elections

World War II Britain. So, to complete our story, Prime Minister Thatcher
showed some savvy in setting the 1983 general election in June, in order to take
advantage of favorable economic conditions.

France

The French experience essentially repeats the patterns established in the British
case. For France, a few voting functions for National Assembly elections have
been proposed (Lewis-Beck and Bellucci 1982; Rosa and Amson 1976). But
overwhelmingly the work is on popularity functions, whose number rivals that
for the American case. Lafay (1985), in his excellent review of them, cites
around fifteen. These efforts accord, in particular, with the contours of the
American work. The dependent variable is always the percentage of the public
who are satisfied with the president (or the prime minister), as measured in a
regular national opinion poll. The macroeconomic variables measure inflation,
unemployment, or income. The noneconomic variables are dummies representing electoral cycles or events. All but one of these many equations uncover
significant economic effects. As a more recent example, here are Lafay's
(1985, table 4, eq. 8, pp. 92–93) estimates (weighted least squares) for the
president (from 1974 to 1983, monthly data):

$$Pt = 1.839 - .028I_{(t-1/6)} - .103U_{(t-1)} + .029G_{(t-1/15)}$$
$$(6.3) \quad (3.4) \qquad (6.6) \qquad (3.1)$$

$$- .253E_{(t-1)} - .310DB + .707DL \qquad\qquad (2.3)$$
$$(6.8) \qquad (4.7) \qquad (7.0)$$
$$R^2 = .77 \quad 104\ df$$

where Pt = proportion of respondents "satisfied" with the president of the
Republic (the logit), in a national poll by Institut Français d'Opinion Publique
(IFOP); $I_{(t-1/6)}$ = inflation rate on six months (lagged by one month), an-
nualized; $U_{(t-1)}$ = unemployment rate, lagged one month; $G_{(t-1/15)}$ = real
disposable income growth on fifteen months (lagged by one month), an-
nualized; $E_{(t-1)}$ = francs per dollar (lagged one month); DB = a dummy
variable for the "Plan Barre" (1 = October, 1976, to January, 1977; 0 =
elsewhere); DL = dummy variable for a leftist administration (1 = June, 1981,
to December, 1983; 0 = elsewhere); the figures in parentheses are t-ratios (|t| >
2 = significance at .05).

These results, as well as those of the other studies, support the notion that
macroeconomic change is related to presidential (and prime minister) support.
Besides this elementary baseline, little can be drawn from the chaotic findings.
As with the British case, disagreement is rife with regard to sampling, mea-

surement, specification, estimation, and evaluation. The data may be monthly (Kernell 1980; Giraud 1980; Lafay 1985; Lafay, Berdot, and Giraud 1981; Lewis-Beck 1980), or quarterly (Hibbs and Vasilatos 1981; Lafay 1973, 1977, 1981a; Lecaillon 1981, 1982), or annual (Lecaillon 1980a, 1980b, 1981). The time periods under study vary. Here, for example, are some different periods for the presidential popularity series: 1965–77 (Lecaillon 1980a); 1960–78 (Lewis-Beck 1980); 1969–78 (Hibbs and Vasilatos 1981); 1974–79 (Giraud 1980); 1974–83 (Lafay 1985).

The problems continue. The three basic economic variables—income, unemployment, inflation—tend to be measured differently from study to study and are not always included together. For instance, as indicators of these three Lafay (1977) utilizes, respectively, a real wage index, the number of unsatisfied employment requests, and the quarterly change in prices. In contrast, Lewis-Beck (1980) looks at the number of unemployed and the rate of change in the consumer price index, but does not include any income measure. With another variant, Hibbs and Vasilatos (1981) focus on the real personal disposable income growth rate. The lag structures of these variables are also quite different. Some investigations posit short, simple lags; e.g., Lewis-Beck (1980) says economic effects are felt after two months. But Hibbs and Vasilatos (1981) argue for a long, elaborate structure of memory in the electorate. Departing from both, Lafay (1985) finds a simple, though different, lag period for each economic variable.

Finally, with regard to the evaluation of the relative importance of the economic effects, there is considerable disagreement. Lafay (1985) attempted to codify these evaluations in the fifteen studies of French popularity to that time. According to his tabulations, the unemployment variable is the most important, using the preliminary standard of statistical significance. More specifically, some version of the unemployment variable registered a statistically significant coefficient (at .05 or more) in thirteen of the fifteen equations. In contrast, inflation and income measures managed significance only nine and seven times, respectively. But if the significance level is made more demanding, the comparison more or less evens out. That is to say, if the .01 level is used, then unemployment is significant only eight times, inflation seven times, and income five times. On the basis of simple, unweighted statistical significance counts, then, it is difficult to sort out which of these factors is more important in determining the popularity of the French executive. Unfortunately, more powerful criteria of evaluation are made difficult by the many differences in measurement and specification across equations.

On top of these uncertainties is an issue that plagues all the studies— popularity at the polls is not equivalent to actual vote support. The political economy connection remains at one remove. While economics may relate to presidential approval, it may not ultimately relate to the vote itself. But in fact, across the presidential elections of the Fifth Republic, it can be shown that macroeconomic performance exhibits a strong association with overall presidential vote. In the equation below, vote support for the presidential incumbent (or his coalition candidate) is predicted (OLS) from the economic growth rate (in the election year).

$$V_t = 46.24 + .018G_t \qquad\qquad (2.4)$$
$$(19.5)\quad (3.9)$$
$$R^2 = .84 \qquad \text{Adj. } R^2 = .78 \qquad N = 5$$

where V_t = second-ballot presidential vote percentage (for the incumbent or his coalition candidate); G_t = growth rate of real GDP (in the election year); the figures in parentheses are t-ratios; $N = 5$ observations, on the presidential elections of 1965, 1969, 1974, 1981, and the 1962 referendum on the direct election of the president (which de Gaulle saw as a referendum on himself).

At least in these few elections, the performance of the economy appears highly predictive of presidential incumbent vote strength (see the pleasing scatterplot in fig. 2.1). An implication is that a sitting president will be returned to office, provided his macroeconomic record appears satisfactory (i.e., more precisely, according to the regression line, he can count on a victory when economic growth clearly exceeds an annual rate of 2 percent). Such a scenario is certainly compatible with the 1988 Mitterrand reelection, where annual growth was moving along at about 2.5 to 3.0 percent going into the contest.

These actual presidential election results, coupled with the many popularity estimates, allow the following limited, but important, conclusion: *in Fifth Republic France, fluctuations in key macroeconomic indicators are associated with electorate support for the president (and the prime minister).*

West Germany

A fair amount of time series research on macroeconomic conditions and electoral outcomes in West Germany has been published, most of it in German and virtually all of it focusing on popularity functions. (See Frey and Garbers 1972; Frey and Schneider 1979, 1980; Kirchgassner 1974, 1977, 1983, 1985a, 1985b, 1985c; Norpoth and Yantek 1983; Peretz 1981; Ronning and Schneider 1976. On vote functions, there is Frey and Weck 1981, on the Weimar Republic from 1930 to 1933; and see Falter and Zintl 1985.) With cues from Goodhart and Bhansali (1970), Kirchgassner (1974) authored the first paper showing a link between economics and popularity in the Federal Republic of Germany. Since then, Kirchgassner has continued to lead the work on the German case. For data, he has relied on monthly polls about the popularity of the two major parties, the Christian Democrats (CDU/CSU) and the Social Democrats (SPD), gathered by the *Institut für Demoskopie in Allensbach*. In

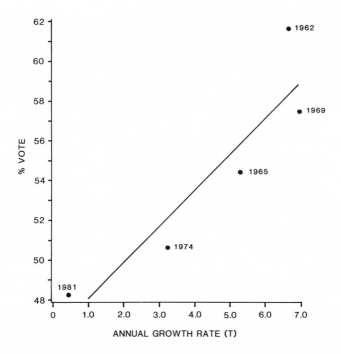

Fig. 2.1. Incumbent French presidential vote and annual economic growth rate in the election year, R^2 = .84. (Data sources: *Annuaire Statistique de la France*, INSEE, Paris; *Main Economic Indicators*, OECD.)

the following typical example are equations for the CDU/CSU, then the SPD, for the Social-Liberal ruling coalition period (Kirchgassner 1985a). The observations are monthly, from January, 1971, to August, 1982, and the estimates are full information, maximum likelihood:

$$C_t = 10.83* + .73*C_{(t-1)} + .34*U_t + .16I_t \qquad (2.5)$$
$$ (5.7) \quad (18.0) \qquad\;\; (4.0) \qquad (1.5)$$
$$ \text{SEE} = 1.60 \qquad h = -.29 \qquad 135\ df$$

$$S_t = 15.15* + .73*S_{(t-1)} - .61*U_t - .40*I_t \qquad (2.6)$$
$$ (6.4) \quad (18.0) \qquad\;\; (-5.4) \quad (-2.9)$$
$$ \text{SEE} = 1.8 \qquad h = .77 \qquad 135\ df$$

where C_t or S_t = the popularity of the Christian Democrats or Social Democrats, as measured in the monthly Allensbach poll data; $C_{(t-1)}$ or $S_{(t-1)}$ = popularity of the parties, lagged one month, respectively; U_t = the seasonally adjusted unemployment rate; I_t = the inflation rate (compared with the same month of the last year); the figures in parentheses are t-ratios; the asterisk (*) indicates significance at .05; h = Durbin's h statistic.

Looking at these results, we see that support for the incumbent party is significantly affected by the unemployment rate and the inflation rate. Further, past preferences of the electorate seem important, as well as current ones, according to the coefficients of $C_{(t-1)}$ and $S_{(t-1)}$, respectively. These two equations show, as does virtually every popularity function estimate for the West German case, that economics matters. Only one recent study contradicts this conclusion. Using Box-Jenkins time series techniques instead of traditional econometric modeling, Norpoth and Yantek (1983) fail to uncover any significant effects of economics on popularity of the parties. However, Kirchgassner (1985b, 1985c), in his own follow-up Box-Jenkins analyses, reaffirmed the importance of the above economic variables. The following generalization, then, seems on firm ground: *increases in the unemployment and inflation rates are associated with decreases in declared public support for the main government party in post–World War II West Germany.*

Italy

With respect to Italy, a few studies are available, but work has been hampered by the complexities of their multiparty system and by the irregular nature of the popularity polling. Italy has more parties than any of the countries under investigation, with the exception of Spain (at least if the regional parties are included; see Lancaster and Lewis-Beck 1985). The party most clearly identified with governing in postwar Italy is the Christian Democratic one. However, it is not so easy to identify the opposition. Is it simply all leftist, fascist, and liberal parties? What about the lesser parties in the incumbent coalition that leave, or threaten to leave? In practice, the papers that have attempted time series models for Italy have selected as the dependent variable either the vote share of the main incumbent party—the Christian Democrats (DC)—or the main opposition party—the Communists (PCI)—which accords with the common "bipartitismo imperfetto" characterization of the system (Lewis-Beck and Bellucci 1982; Bellucci 1984). Here is the Lewis-Beck and Bellucci (1982, 100) voting function (OLS estimates) for the Communist party, in national legislative elections from 1953 to 1979:

$$C_t = 24.87 - .49U_{(t-1)} + .76F_{(t-1)} \qquad (2.7)$$
$$(-2.3) \qquad (8.1)$$
$$R^2 = .94 \qquad N = 7 \qquad DW = 2.7$$

where C_t = the percentage of the total vote in the national legislative election won by the Communist party; $U_{(t-1)}$ = the unemployment rate the prior year;

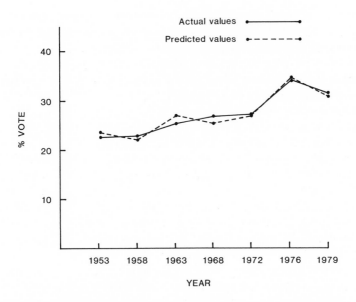

Fig. 2.2. Predicting the Italian Communist party vote. (Data sources: see definitions for eq. 2.7.)

$F_{(t-1)}$ = the inflation rate the prior year; the figures in parentheses below the coefficients are t-ratios (if $|t| > 2.35$, then the coefficient is significant at .05, one-tail). The vote data are from Chris Cook and John Paxton, *European Political Facts: 1918–1973* (New York: St. Martin's Press, 1975); updated from *European Journal of Political Research*, various issues. The economic data are from B. R. Mitchell, *European Historical Statistics: 1950–1970* (New York: Columbia University Press, 1975); updated from *Main Economic Indicators*, OECD, various issues.

On the basis of these estimates, *the Communist vote share fluctuates predictably according to macroeconomic change.* Figure 2.2 shows how closely the predicted votes track the actual. Changes in inflation and unemployment foretell changes in the Communist vote. More particularly, a 1 percent rise in inflation is associated with a 0.75 percent rise in the PCI vote share. And a 1 percent jump in unemployment is followed by a 0.5 percent decline in the PCI vote share.

Can this model be used to predict future elections? The high R^2 argues for its forecasting potential, but the small sample size counsels caution. How does the model fare when used to forecast more recent lower house elections? Going into the election of June, 1987, scores on the predictor variables of unemployment and inflation were, respectively, about 14 percent and 4 percent (*Econo-*

mist, June 13, 1987, 113). These figures of high unemployment and low inflation predict a sizable decline in PCI support. In fact, this is what happened. The Communist party experienced a net loss of twenty-one seats, falling to their lowest level of support in twenty years. The model, then, does have some predictive ability. However, substantively, it offers a "perverse" explanation of economic effects on the Italian voter.

That is to say, the negative sign for the unemployment variable goes against the usual political economy hypothesis, implying instead that adverse economic conditions (e.g., rising unemployment) cause voters to punish the opposition (e.g., decrease the Communist vote). Such an anomalous finding illustrates well the central difficulty of aggregate data analysis—making inferences to individual behavior. If one takes the unemployment coefficient literally, it suggests that the unemployed are more likely to vote for, say, incumbent Christian Democrats. This possibility seems improbable. But what does seem probable is that some third factor is operating on the aggregate data, thus allowing this spurious inference to individual voters. More pointedly, we know that urban areas are more Communist in Italy than rural areas and that urban areas have lower rates of unemployment (Galli and Prandi 1970; Sani 1978). This common prior influence of urbanization is responsible for most, if not all, of the unexpected relationship one observes between the unemployment rate and the Communist vote in equation 2.7. (This pattern of influence is diagramed in fig. 2.3.)

The work on Italian popularity functions, carried out exclusively by Santagata (1981, 1982), is more consistent with a standard political economy hypothesis. But before considering his results, it is necessary to mention the formidable data obstacles to the construction of popularity functions for Italy, obstacles that Santagata (1982, 21) fully appreciates. The polling firm, Istituto Doxa, has posed the following question in national surveys: "What do you think about the way the Prime Minister Mr. ——— does his job?" Unfortunately, the question has been rarely asked. In fact, from 1960 to 1981, only eighteen such polls are available, thus forming a fragile base for analysis. Santagata (1982) relates the percentage of those approving of the prime minister to various economic variables (measured for the quarter in which the survey took place). Here is his OLS equation linking prime minister popularity to inflation, unemployment, and real income (Santagata 1982, 22):

$$P = 47.3 - 1.4*F_{(t)} + 1.0U_{(t)} + .83N_{(t)} \qquad (2.8)$$
$$(4.4) \quad (3.92) \qquad (.5) \quad (1.20)$$
$$\text{Adj. } R^2 = .73 \qquad N = 17 \qquad DW = 1.63$$

where P = the percentage of those polled (excluding "don't knows") who approve of the way the prime minister does his job ("approve totally" plus

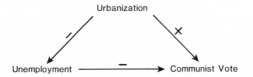

Fig. 2.3.   The aggregate relationship of urbanization to unemployment and the Communist party vote in Italy

"worked rather well"); $F_{(t)}$ = the rate of change in the cost-of-living index, not lagged; $U_{(t)}$ = the unemployment rate, not lagged; $N_{(t)}$ = yearly change of real income; the figures in parentheses under the coefficients are t-ratios; the asterisk (*) = statistically significant at .05.

These results show that a rising inflation rate is significantly associated with a decline in prime minister popularity, but unemployment and income changes are not. But these results, and those from slightly different specifications, are suspect because of the problem of high multicollinearity among the economic variables, a difficulty encountered by Lewis-Beck and Bellucci (1982, 100) as well. Thus, Santagata (1982, 24) goes on to show that the economic variables, when regressed separately on popularity, easily demonstrate significance. Moreover, when placed at a one-year lag, the fit is improved. His two "best" equations, then, consist of simple regressions, one with popularity a function of a lagged inflation rate, another with popularity a function of a lagged unemployment rate (Santagata 1982, 24).

These findings imply that either inflation or unemployment is capable of influencing the popularity of the prime minister, who was always a Christian Democrat during the period under study. Rising unemployment, as well as rising prices, appear to lower support for the incumbent, a result which is consistent with the political economy hypothesis but contradicts the Italian vote functions. What can we conclude about the Italian case? Little can be said with much assurance, given the small amount of work that has been done and the peculiar complications of the Italian setting. Certainly, though, it is safe to say that the notion of the economy affecting the electorate has not been ruled out.

Spain

Until very recently, Spain was not fertile ground for aggregate time series studies of economic conditions and electoral outcomes. The renewed Spanish democracy, with national elections just begun in 1977, provides too few data points to construct the usual vote function. It is of more than passing interest, however, that an incumbent Democratic Center Union (UCD) party fell from a national election vote share of 35 percent in 1979 to just a 7 percent share in 1982, in the face of an accompanying rise in the unemployment rate from 9 percent to 17 percent. Indeed, Lancaster (1984) directly attributes the 1982 UCD defeat to this climb in unemployment. In the general election of June, 1986, the ruling Socialist government of Felipe Gonzáles experienced a net loss of eighteen seats in the Cortes, perhaps because of an unemployment rate that reached 21 percent. But this is anecdotal evidence. Fortunately, more systematic work on popularity functions has become available.

Amor Bravo (1985, 1986, 1987) has developed a Spanish popularity function that follows along the theoretical lines traveled by other European political economists. In his most recent paper, several specifications are offered and estimated. The equation on quarterly data from 1976 to 1985 is perhaps typical (Amor Bravo 1987, 203–6, see eq. 5, cuadro 1):

Economic Variables
$$P = 1.33U + 1.14F + 3.9*I$$
$$\quad (1.3) \quad\ (2.0) \quad\ (4.7)$$

Political Variables
$$+31.7AS1 + 8.8AS2 + 1.9CS + 14.5FG$$
$$\quad (2.0) \qquad (5.2) \qquad (3.6) \qquad (1.4)$$

Depreciation Variable
$$-7.2D \hfill (2.9)$$
$$\ (7.0)$$
$$R^2 = .88 \qquad DW = 2.12 \qquad 29\ df$$

where P = the percentage popularity of the president, measured by Gallup; U = the unemployment rate; F = inflation rate (based on consumer prices); I = real income growth rate; AS1, AS2, CS, and FG are dummy variables, representing the popularity level of each government associated with the president during that period (Adolfo Suárez, Calvo Sotelo, Felipe González); D = a depreciation variable that captures the decline of the UCD party; the figures in parentheses are t-ratios; the asterisk (*) = a statistically significant economic variable, at .05 in the expected direction.

These results suggest that increases in real income enhance the popularity of the Spanish president. On the basis of this (and other) estimations, Amor Bravo (1987, 204) concludes that income has an "influencia indudable," while inflation and unemployment do not. Thus, the Spanish result accords, in at least a general way, with presidential popularity functions from the other nations. No case for "Spanish exceptionalism" appears necessary. This should encourage further work on government popularity functions, as well as on vote functions.

The United States

Out of all the nations under study, aggregate time series work on the United States is the most voluminous and the best known. Also, it has been heavily reviewed (most recently, on vote functions, see Kiewiet and Rivers 1984; on popularity functions, see Norpoth 1984). Fortunately, as with the French case, it can be demonstrated that popularity in the polls is highly related to actual incumbent vote totals (Brody and Sigelman 1983; Lewis-Beck 1985a; Lewis-Beck and Rice 1982). Therefore, I concentrate on vote functions, briefly summarizing the main findings on the congressional election work begun by Kramer (1971), and then providing illustrative current models.

Kramer's (1971) article launched, and continues to influence, the contemporary debate about the role of economics in American elections. He argued that if voters find the economic performance of the president's party "satisfactory," they vote for that party in a congressional election; otherwise, they vote for an opposition party (131). To test his model, Kramer turned to national observations on House of Representative elections, from 1896 to 1964 (excluding the problematic years 1912, 1918, 1942, and 1944). According to his original OLS estimates, while neither the inflation nor the unemployment variables managed to attain conventional levels of statistical significance, the income variable did so handily. Further, he concluded that the effects of income shifts were important; i.e., a 10 percent drop in real per capita personal income would cost the president's party about 5 percent of the congressional vote (140–41).

Kramer's (1971) work quickly drew fire, mostly from economists who doubted that it was "rational" for voters to act in that way and who set out to prove it (Stigler 1973; Arcelus and Meltzer 1975). In response to these criticisms, Kramer and Goodman re-worked Kramer's model, finding that actually each of the economic variables—income, inflation, unemployment—manifests a statistically significant connection to voting for Congress (Goodman and Kramer 1975, 1,263). Thus, they strengthened the original position, concluding that "all three economic variables do influence congressional elections" (Goodman and Kramer 1975, 1,264).

The general notion that economics shapes legislative elections was soon reinforced by Tufte (1975, 1978), and then by Hibbs (1982b). Tufte (1975), making his own start from a somewhat different perspective, developed an uncomplicated model for midterm congressional elections that seemed both statistically and theoretically convincing. He argued that midterm House races were, as politicians claimed, referenda on the performance of the president's

[handwritten note at bottom of page] Could rising polarization in a given country lead to less economic voting? → given levels of partisanship...

analyzed midterm elections in the House (handwritten margin note)

party, with the voters responding according to economic and noneconomic issues. The economic condition that induces change in a standardized midterm vote measure is the election year change in real disposable income per capita. In order to capture the influence of noneconomic issues, he included the variable of presidential approval, measured by Gallup right before the election. This straightforward model, estimated with OLS over the eight midterm House elections from 1946 to 1974, produced highly significant coefficients and an impressive goodness-of-fit statistic (Tufte 1978, 112).

in Gov't and affect (handwritten margin note)

Tufte's compelling work has provided a direction for much subsequent congressional election modeling. (On the House, see Campbell 1986; Jacobson and Kernell 1983; Lewis-Beck and Rice 1984; Oppenheimer, Stimson, and Waterman 1986; Witt 1983. On the Senate, see Abramowitz and Segal 1986; Hibbing and Alford 1982; Lewis-Beck and Rice 1985a.) Here is a recent example, from Lewis-Beck and Rice (1984), up-dated to include results through 1984.

$$S = -72.3 + .84*P_{(t-6)} + 7.47*G_{(t-6)} + 24.1*D \qquad \textbf{(2.10)}$$
$$(4.66) \qquad (3.07) \qquad (4.97)$$
$$R^2 = .84 \qquad SEE = 10.89 \qquad N = 18$$

where S = House seats gained or lost by the president's party; $P_{(t-6)}$ = Gallup presidential popularity in May of the election year; $G_{(t-6)}$ = growth rate of real GNP in the second quarter of the election year; D = midterm dummy (0 = midterm; 1 = presidential election year); the figures in parentheses = t-ratios; the asterisk (*) = significant at .05; $N = 18$ observations (1950–84).

According to these OLS estimates, net incumbent seat changes in the House are determined by presidential popularity, the economic growth rate, and the electoral calender (midterm or not). The economic impact appears statistically and substantively significant; i.e., a 1 percent increase in GNP is associated with a seven-and-one-half seat gain for the incumbent party.

Hence, the general argument for the presence of economic effects is clearly supported, even in the face of the rather dramatic differences in model specification posed by Kramer, Tufte, and their followers. The case for the economic-electoral connection is further strengthened by the work of Hibbs (most recently, see 1987). His choices about data and measures for congressional voting functions are in some ways similar to Tufte; i.e., the post–World War II period is chosen, the dependent variable is the same, and the economic variable of choice is income. However, he argues that voters evaluate income performance geometrically, with performance closer to the election weighted more heavily than that earlier in the term. Further, this is the sole factor, economic or noneconomic. Here is a Hibbs model for midterm House elections from 1946 to 1978 (Hibbs 1982, 410):

$$V = -3.15 + .93 \left[\sum_{i=0}^{5} .34R^i_{t-i-2} \left(1/\sum_{i=0}^{5} .34^i\right) \right] \qquad \textbf{(2.11)}$$

$$(.55) \quad (.21) \qquad\qquad (.11)$$
$$R^2 = .76 \qquad \text{SEE} = 1.53 \qquad N = 9$$

where V = standardized vote loss, the midterm House vote percentage for the president's party less the average aggregate vote percentage for his party in previous elections; R in brackets = the geometrically weighted average income term, defined as in the above paragraph; the figures in parentheses beneath the coefficients are standard errors.

The Hibbs model, taken at face value, suggests a position of near economic determinism for congressional election outcomes. Hibbs, himself, has implied as much: "The electoral success of President Reagan and the Republicans in 1984 does hinge on an improvement—in fact, a very sharp improvement—in current economic conditions" (Hibbs 1982, 413). *However, one does not need to be an economic determinist to appreciate the thrust of the American research on congressional vote functions: economics matters.*

Summary and Conclusions

In this chapter I have offered a purposeful critique of aggregate time series studies of economics and elections in six leading Western democracies—Britain, France, Germany, Italy, Spain, and the United States. Despite the cultural and institutional differences that distinguish these nations, some clear patterns emerge. Economics and elections are joined. This judgment is statistically quite secure. The number of vote and popularity functions reported for these countries now numbers well over one hundred. All but a handful find that economic conditions are significantly related to electoral outcomes. *One conclusion is unambiguous: macroeconomic downturn is associated with a fall in government support.*

This is a noteworthy finding. Still, many questions remain unanswered in this large body of aggregate time series studies. First, how should the universe be sampled? Some studies select monthly observations, others quarterly or annual. The time period may reach back to the nineteenth century or stop at World War II. War years may be excluded. The sample frame might be dictated by the value on a third variable, e.g., the administration in office or the general economic climate. Second, how should the model be specified? Certain studies include noneconomic variables such as partisanship, electoral cycles, or major events, while others do not. With regard to the economic variables, the common ones are income, unemployment, and inflation. But they are not always included together. And a few investigations have proposed quite different economic variables, e.g., the balance of trade. Third, how are the economic variables actually to be measured? Different indicators for the same conceptual variable (e.g., unemployment) are available, and they have been treated as levels, changes, or changes of changes. Further, the lag structures vary widely, from no lag to elaborate distributed or geometric lags. Finally, how important are economic forces relative to the other factors that impact on the electorate?

In my view, these central issues are not likely to be resolved by further analyses of national aggregates. Why? Almost every model reviewed, different as it may be from the next, can claim theoretical and statistical support from some corner. Still, let us suppose that agreement were reached on the sampling, the measures, and the model, which was then properly estimated and evaluated. Such serendipity would not get at a fundamental problem of these aggregate data: they do not tell us about the behavior of individual voters. *What gives meaning to the foregoing statistical associations between economics and elections is the underlying belief that individual citizens react systematically to economic stimuli at the ballot box. But is this the case?*

Certainly, if voters do so act, then the observed general association between macroeconomic conditions and incumbent vote totals would be expected. Still, rival individual level processes could be responsible for this observed aggregate time series association. For example, in years of recession, the incumbent party may run poor candidates, on the theory that they, rather than the good candidates, should risk electoral sacrifice. Then, voters will be more likely to vote against the incumbent party, simply because they are fielding poorer candidates. (Jacobson [1983, chap. 6] makes this argument especially well.) However, in the aggregate statistics, such candidate-motivated defection from the incumbent will show up as a correlation between economics and elections, with the spurious implication that the economic downturn is directly causing this incumbent vote loss. Moreover, *even if we assume that the aggregate level correlation is not spurious, the results give few guidelines about individual economic voting.* What economic conditions do voters look at? Is that looking passionate or dispassionate? Retrospective or prospective? Simple or complex? How important are these economic concerns compared to other factors operating on the voter?

To overcome the risk of making faulty inferences from the nation to the citizen (the familiar ecological fallacy), various strategies have been pursued. One approach has been to disaggregate to a lower geographic unit of analysis. For instance, Owens and Olson (1980) examined aggregate political and economic indicators of U.S. congressional districts, instead of the nation as a whole. In Italy, Bellucci (1984) conducted a time series analysis region by region. Another tactic is merely to use aggregate models to *forecast* election results, rather than *explain* them. This perspective has been adopted in predicting British and French legislative election outcomes (see Lewis-Beck 1985a, 1986a; Mughan 1987). A current angle, which is perhaps only feasible with the bountiful data of the American case, combines traditional aggregate time series with election survey data. In this regard, Markus (1988) and Rivers (1988) have generated some interesting, if contradictory, results on the "Kramer problem" (Kramer 1983).

Another approach, the one followed in part 2, involves cross-national analysis of comparable individual-level surveys, namely, the special Euro-Barometer surveys that were administered twice (1983 and 1984) to the electorates of Britain, France, Germany, Italy, and Spain. *Analysis of these surveys offers an important advantage over the work reviewed in this chapter: the electoral preferences of individual citizens are the direct focus of investigation.* This permits an answer to many of the still-unanswered questions. And there is a second, equally important, advantage. Virtually all previous research has gone forward on a single-country basis. That is, each researcher formulates a model for just one nation (usually his or her homeland). While the work may be comparative at some theoretical level, the actual models are invariably idiosyncratic to a particular country. (The sole exception here is Paldam; see Paldam 1981b, 1986.) Thus, model-building and systematic accumulation of evidence have been greatly slowed. In what follows, *I propose a model of economic voting, then test it across the five nations using the same measures.* Hopefully, this gets us closer to the real similarities (and differences) in the economics-election connection as it operates for these leading Western democracies.

NOTE

1. Economically driven popularity functions have been developed for the smaller democracies, as well as the major ones considered here. Here are some examples: Australia (Schneider and Pommerehne 1980); Denmark (Paldam and Schneider 1980); Sweden (Sigelman 1983).

Chapter 3

Economic Voting: Theory and Measurement in the European Surveys

Si les élections se jouent contra la majorité actuelle, ce sera à cause du chômage. (President Mitterrand, *Centre Presse*, Vienne, December 10, 1985, p. 23)

If economics influences elections, then individual citizens must receive economic stimuli and respond to them nonrandomly in the polling place. How does this work? In the popular view, the mechanism is pocketbook voting. That is, the voter aims to enhance his or her material self-interest. This axiom, articulated in different ways at various levels of sophistication, has been argued for a long time, from Adam Smith to Anthony Downs. Its staying power comes as much as anything from its intuitive appeal. But does research support this intuition? For an answer, scholars have studied individuals. The exclusive vehicle for these individual studies has been election surveys, almost all from the United States. (One exception is the Rattinger 1981 study on Germany.) This research has made the pocketbook voting assumption much less self-evident. Therefore, it is a good idea to be more explicit about voting theory. A prerequisite here is Fiorina's (1981) excellent general treatment. His work is much inspired by V. O. Key, who provided a powerful theoretical direction for much of the economic voting research:

> The patterns of flow of the major streams of shifting voters graphically reflect the electorate in its great, and perhaps principal, role as an appraiser of past events, past performance, and past actions. It judges retrospectively . . . . Voters may reject what they have known; or they may approve what they have known. They are not likely to be attracted in great numbers by promises . . . . (Key 1966, 61).

Several of these points deserve emphasis. Voters make judgments. They make them about "past events, past performance, and past actions." On the basis of these retrospective judgments, they vote to "reject" or "approve." Thus, voters are not blind subjects of sociological forces. Nor are they tabulae

33

rasae, waiting to be filled with campaign promises. Rather, voters weigh how things have been and act accordingly.

How does this express itself specifically as economic voting? Butler and Stokes (1969, 392), in their comprehensive study of political change in Britain, describe it well:

> The electorate's response to the economy is one under which voters reward the Government for the conditions they welcome and punish the Government for the conditions they dislike. In the simplest of all such models the electorate pays attention only to the party in power and only to conditions during its current tenure in office.

Allow me to restate this a bit to make it more applicable to democratic systems generally, and let the proposition represent *traditional economic voting theory*:

> When voters approve (disapprove) of past economic conditions, they vote for (against) the governing party (or parties).

What is the precise meaning of this proposition? First, what is the economic object of attention? The pocketbook voter research assumes it is the individual (or family). However, in evaluating economic conditions, the voter may be primarily focusing on a larger social entity, such as the nation. Second, what is the actual time horizon? Traditional theory assumes voters look to the economic past, but perhaps they are more interested in the economic future. Third, how do voters arrive at their judgments? Are their assessments straightforward or convoluted? Are voters as calculating as the above implies, or do they react with passion? In this chapter, I first examine these conceptual issues and then consider the measurement requirements. After that, I offer preliminary distribution and correlation results on the chosen measures, from the Euro-Barometer national surveys in Britain, France, Germany, Italy, and Spain.

Self versus Society

We do not know as much as we would like about how citizens mentally process economic events. But it is a cinch that few formally utilize macroeconomic models, price theory, or statistics. Instead, they most likely "morselize" economics, just as they do politics (Lane 1962). That is, citizens tend to consider only pieces of the economic puzzle, largely in isolation from one another. They think about grocery bills, car loans, their daughter's college, and the amount of money they have to cover these expenses. Such personal financial concerns do appear to have some impact on American voters, at least when they are choosing a president. (The results on House elections suggest no effect; see especially Fiorina 1978, 434-36.) This conclusion has survived repeated testing under different model specifications, election years, data, and estimation procedures. The exhaustive probit analyses of Kiewiet (1983, 49) suggest that, on average, voters who believe their personal financial situation has gotten better are 13 percent more likely to support the incumbent party in presidential elections, when compared to those who believe their financial situation has gotten worse. More recently, Markus (1988), employing an instrumental variables approach, arrives at a similar estimate.

Personal Economic Concerns

In the Euro-Barometer surveys, the basic question for measuring personal economic situation is as follows:

> How does the financial situation of your household now compare with what it was 12 months ago? (lot better, better, same, little worse, worse).

This measure compares to the standard U.S. National Election Study (NES) item on personal finances, with the important qualification that it has five categories, rather than the usual three (better, same, worse). This modification is in line with the recommendations of Rosenstone, Hansen, and Kinder (1983). As part of a Center for Political Studies (CPS) Pilot Survey for the 1984 NES, they explored at least five distinct measures of personal economic well-being. An important conclusion is that a five-point personal financial situation item out-performs the traditional three-point item. In fact, they estimate that the use "of the traditional better/worse off financially question causes one to underestimate, by as much as one-half, the political effect of personal economic conditions" (Rosenstone, Hansen, and Kinder 1983, 14).

Pocketbook voting also seems more detectable under particular circumstances. Specifically, the perceptions of economic responsibility held by the voter can play a role (see Peffley 1984). Consider the mental process that might appear required at minimum for a citizen, say Jane Doe, consciously to vote just on her pocketbook: (1) she perceives that her financial situation has changed; (2) she praises or blames the incumbent party (or party representative) for that change; (3) she votes for or against that party in the next election.

Obviously, the key link in this logical chain is the second step, the attribution of responsibility for the economic change to the incumbent party. Put another way, if Jane believes that her altered financial situation (e.g., a job loss) has nothing to do with politics (e.g., the Republican administration), then it makes little sense for her to respond with a Democratic vote in the upcoming election. Such a vote, to be "rational," demands as a preliminary step that she accuse the Republicans of bringing about her economic plight. If most citizens attribute personal financial fortune to individual initiative, a generous boss, or good luck, rather than to politics or society, then only a weak association between personal economic well-being and the vote would be expected.

In their work, Brody and Sniderman (1977) offered evidence that Americans tend to assign responsibility for personal problems to themselves, rather than to larger social entities. Relatedly, Schlozman and Verba (1979, 194) found that those who had lost their jobs "did not see themselves as victims of broad social forces or governmental ineptitude but of specific events connected with their particular employment circumstances." With such attitudes, individual hardships would remain unpoliticized. Indeed, Feldman (1982, 449), in his survey analysis of American elections, offers support for the following specific hypothesis: "Personal economic conditions will influence voting behavior only when there is a perception of social (economic, governmental) responsibility for financial well-being." One difficulty with this provocative finding is that it is based on only one election year, 1972. However, his conclusions are bolstered by Kinder and Mebane's (1983) study of presidential voting from 1956 to 1976. They isolated voters who explained their economic circumstances in a nonpersonal way from those who did not. In each of the elections (with the exception of 1964), the association between the personal financial situation variable and presidential vote was stronger in the first group, which assigned responsibility for their economic predicament to societal factors.

The foregoing research reinforces the notion that the strength of pocketbook voting depends on the development of a particular pattern of causal reasoning about the responsibility for personal economic conditions. For instance, family financial losses must be blamed not on family error, but on larger social forces that politics might conceivably impinge upon. Of course, such a pattern of causal attribution (or its absence) is not immutable in the minds of voters. On one hand, in times of severe economic recession, voters might be led to make these mental connections rather easily. On the other hand, in times of economic boom, voters may follow a psychological tendency to credit themselves with success, seldom consciously associating their well-being with politics (Weiner et al. 1972). Given these considerations, it seemed advisable to include in the European surveys a direct item permitting citizens to attribute responsibility to government for their personal financial situation, as follows:

> Compared with a year ago, would you say that the government's policies have had a good effect, a bad effect, or that they really have not made much difference with regard to the financial situation of your household?

It is important to mention that this question, along with all the other economic items eventually inserted into the surveys, were placed at a considerable distance from the dependent variable of vote. (In Euro-Barometer No. 21, almost two hundred places separate the economic questions from the vote question.) This was done as a precaution, in order to avoid possible artifactual effects from item proximity. In particular, Sears and Lau (1983) have contended that most of the positive findings on pocketbook effects in the American literature can be accounted for by the close proximity of political and economic questions in the surveys. According to the argument, in such a circumstance, voters try to "rationalize" their responses, making them more consistent.

The Sears and Lau argument raises fundamental concerns about the use of surveys for the study of economic voting, not to mention for the study of electoral behavior in general. However, when I tested their hypothesis directly on the CPS-SRC surveys (1956–82) themselves, I found no such artifact (Lewis-Beck 1985b). In particular, despite various specifications, I failed to uncover a statistically significant relationship between the closeness of the standard personal finances item, C (measured by the number of questions in between), and the strength of personal economic voting, S. Nevertheless, since Sears and Lau (1983) do demonstrate that the artifact can be induced in experimental tests, it seemed prudent to take the opportunity to separate the two sets of items in the special Euro-Barometers conducted in 1983 and 1984.[1]

Collective Economic Concerns

While the pocketbook might be counted on to deliver some legislative votes, the rather modest effects discovered for the U.S. case imply that economic voters have other important objects of evaluation. Specifically, these voters must regard the economics of "society," as well as the economics of "self." They see how their neighbors are doing, hear about local plant closings, and read of the nation's prosperity in the paper. This economic information is distilled into impressions about how economic collectives—the community, the state, the nation—are faring. What is the electoral impact of these collective economic judgments? For example, if voters perceive that the national economy has declined, do they vote against the government, as traditional theory would suggest? Yes, at least according to research on the United States.

In their important works on the topic, Kinder and Kiewiet have argued that American economic voters are more likely to ask of government, "What have you done for the *country* lately?" rather than "What have you done for *me* lately?" (Kinder and Mebane 1983). Thus, the strong motivation is collective or "sociotropic," as they call it, rather than personal or "pocketbook" (Kinder and Kiewiet 1981). (Of course, sociotropic voters are not necessarily altruists. Rather, they may simply believe that their interests are ultimately better served when the collectivity prospers.)

The United States survey evidence supports the Kinder and Kiewiet conjecture. The pivotal CPS-SRC survey item for measuring collective judgments is one that assesses the national "business conditions." When placed in multivariate models with appropriate controls and made to compete head-on against items on personal financial well-being, this national business conditions item is usually a much stronger vote predictor (Kinder and Kiewiet 1979, 1981). Among voters who perceive that the nation's business conditions had worsened over the past year, there is a greater tendency to vote against candidates of the incumbent party.

This conclusion appears generalizable across the congressional and presidential elections for which survey data are available. Kiewiet (1983, 95–108), in an exhaustive treatment, mines the CPS-SRC data from 1958 to 1980. In the probit estimation of carefully specified presidential voting models, when the national business condition variable is present it is statistically significant (with the exception of one election). Further, it is substantively significant, for "the effect upon voting decisions registered by these measures was impressive in magnitude" (99). With respect to the congressional level, the pattern is similar, although the strength of the effect is somewhat diminished (102–7). Overall, his results suggest that collective economic voting, when compared directly to pocketbook voting, manages to account for about twice the variation in presidential and congressional voting (Kiewiet and Rivers 1984).

Collective judgments about the national economy definitely seem worth measuring. Here is the Euro-Barometer item, constructed to parallel the U.S. one:

> How do you think the general economic situation in this country has changed over the last 12 months? (lot better, better, same, little worse, worse).

It is instructive to speculate on the mental steps that lead the voter from national economic observation to political action. What cognitive paths might form the basis of this connection? For the sociotropic voter, the national government is expected to manage the economy, which makes voters quick to punish the incumbent party for failing economic performance. Baldly put, a voter who sees escalating nationwide unemployment places the blame with the current administration, then ballots against it. If this is indeed the way sociotropic voters mentally link economics and elections, then perhaps these processes should receive greater recognition in the survey items. For instance, instead of simply asking the above question, something like the following item should also be posed:

Compared with a year ago, would you say that the government's policies have had a good effect, a bad effect, or that they really have not made much difference with regard to the country's general economic situation?

The earlier question is "simple" in structure. It requests the respondent to make a rough judgment about a single, reasonably familiar, economic object—general economic conditions. This question here is "complex." It asks for judgments about two sets of objects—general economic conditions and government policy—the second being less familiar. Moreover, the question insists that the respondent systematically relate the two. (These distinctions between "simple" and "complex" evaluations are similar, but not identical, to those made by Fiorina [1981, 80–81, 106–29] for "simple" and "mediated" evaluations.) Between these simple and complex questions, the key difference, of course, involves making the government connection explicit. The obvious gain from the administration of complex items is that they incorporate at least the bare bones of the logic of sociotropic voting.

If that logic is in fact widely practiced by voters, then complex items should demonstrate a stronger relationship to the vote than simple items (provided they are essentially the same items in other respects). Such appears to be the case, on the basis of some U.S. results (see Fiorina 1981, 29–31). The suggestion is that complex questions, i.e., those that make the government-economy link explicit, are generally better predictors of vote choice than are simple questions. Clearly, though, these complex questions are more at risk for voter rationalization. In particular, the direct governmental cues in the above item may lead respondents to react as if this were a party preference question, causing them to give partisan answers. For instance, Juan Diego in Spain may say that the economic policies of the Socialist government are having a "good effect" just because he is a Socialist and supports González.

What is essential in the survey instrumentation, then, is to remove the potentially distorting influences of partisanship. When this has been done with American data, one observes that such complex collective economic judgments are much more than mere partisan rationalization (Kinder and Kiewiet 1979, 1981). Even after imposing a statistical control for party identification, the strength of government economic policy evaluation comes through clearly. In order to reach a full understanding of economic voting, it seems necessary to include such complex questions.

Past versus Future

According to traditional theory, economic voters dwell upon past conditions in making their evaluations. The retrospective stance has much to recommend it. Voters are assumed to focus on fact, not fantasy. That is, they judge what the incumbent party has accomplished, not what it promises to accomplish. Thus, votes are cast on the basis of economic performance, rather than economic policy proposals. This makes the standard for rational voter choice more realistic. For instance, with regard to the unemployment problem, the citizen does not need to decide whether the proper strategy is public spending, job retraining, tax incentives, or whatever. He or she merely needs to make a judgment about whether unemployment has been at an acceptable level. If the answer is no, chances of a proincumbent vote go down. Such voting bodes well for the democratic process, because it means that politicians who do not deliver valued results are held accountable at election time.

Retrospective voting theory is all very fine, but it is not what we were taught in civics class. There the idea was that the competing candidates made promises about what they would do if elected, and the voters cast ballots for the set of promises they preferred. In other words, a fair amount of thought and study was required in order to weigh the alternatives and arrive at a decision. Further, that decision was purely prospective. Which is to say, the voter acted on the basis of what the candidates said they were going to do, not what they had done. Does this "civic" voter exist only in the land of Arcadia? Do economic voters put aside their hopes for the future when they are in the voting booth? Some limited research suggests otherwise (the time horizon of American voters is fully investigated, with new data, in chap. 8).

While virtually all aggregate time series studies have employed a retrospective model, this is in part encouraged by the chronological nature of the data (for an important exception, see Chappell and Keech 1985). Nevertheless, Kramer (1971, 134), in his initial investigation, gave consideration to the future orientation of voters, remarking on their "expectations about year t." His notions were inspired by the role Downs (1957) gives to future expectations in his model of the rational voter. According to Downs, "When a man votes, he is helping to select the government which will govern him during the coming election period . . . . He makes his decision by comparing future performances he expects from the competing parties" (39). A scattering of United States election survey studies have explored the role of prospective evaluations. After his examination of CPS-SRC surveys for the 1974 and 1976 elections, Fiorina (1981, 164–75) concedes that future economic expectations can have an important impact on the vote. Further, Kuklinski and West (1981), in their exploration of the 1978 CPS-SRC election study, find that an orientation to the economic future can influence congressional vote choice, at least in Senate races. With regard to Europe, Alt's (1984) work on Britain is unique. He concludes: "it is not enough for incumbents to campaign on their achievements, . . . they have as well to create situations in which people are confident of the future" (329). Certainly, the place of prospective, as well as retrospective, economic voting in all these European electorates merits serious investigation. The central survey item employed to tap prospective economic evaluation in the special Euro-Barometers is as follows:

> Do you think that, a year from now, the government's policies will have improved the country's general economic situation, will have made it worse, or that they will not have made much difference one way or another?

Cognitive versus Affective

Formal considerations of the decision-making processes of the economic voter invariably posit a rational actor model, à la Downs (1957). The voter is portrayed as a logical and efficient calculator who carefully weighs the economic performance (realized or expected) of the different parties, then chooses the one that yields the most benefits. Many voters may behave this way, and in any case the model has proved a valuable heuristic. Still, it neglects the emotional side of life. What about feelings, sentiments, passions? These factors certainly seem to dominate important areas of decision-making, at least for many Americans. They marry for love, not for money. On Sunday mornings, they go to church, instead of stay in bed. During the World Series, they cheer for the underdog. We know that passion can fill politics as well. But does it influence the prosaic act of voting, especially economic voting? Are those who express anger over their declining income more likely to vote against the government than those who merely judge their income to be falling? Or to take a collective example, is a citizen who voices hope about the nation's economic progress more likely to vote for the administration than someone who just notes that key macroeconomic indicators seem to be moving in the right direction? Perhaps, though, these cognitive and affective expressions come to the same thing, both registering, respectively, one type of cost (benefit) that can alter the probability of an anti-incumbent vote. Not so, according to Conover and Feldman (1986), who argue that there are independent cognitive and affective dimensions to economic voting.

For Conover and Feldman, an affective interpretation of economic events differs from a purely cognitive (i.e., rational information-processing) interpretation and leads to a changed perceptual structure and a different vote outcome (they draw supporting social-psychological theory from Fiske and Taylor 1984 and Zajonc 1980, among others). They tested their ideas in a three-wave telephone survey of 915 respondents, administered in Lexington, Kentucky, during 1982 and 1983. The measure of emotional response to the economy was adopted from the affect checklist, first employed in the 1980 Michigan National Election Study for application to political candidates (Abelson et al. 1981). The list included five negative emotions—angry, afraid, disgusted, frustrated, uneasy—and five positive emotions—hopeful, proud, happy, sympathetic, confident. They were applied to the economy in the following way in the survey, e.g., "In the last six months, has the nation's economy made you feel angry? . . . hopeful? . . . disgusted? . . ." and so on through the list. In addition, a set of more or less standard cognitive items assessing personal financial situation and the national economy (inflation, unemployment, the Dow Jones average, the tax cut) were included, along with the usual sociodemographic and partisan control variables. For dependent variables, different questions were asked about President Reagan's performance.

Conover and Feldman explored several questions and estimated several equations. First, one observes the expected. That is, party identification is the strongest predictor of support for President Reagan's handling of the economy. In addition, cognitive evaluations of national economic performance are significant determinants, especially the assessment of inflation. What surprises is the independent impact of the affective evaluations. Positive feelings about how the economy has been doing—hope, pride, confidence, happiness— significantly influence the voters' rating of President Reagan, quite apart from any more reserved evaluation that reason alone may have led them to. Also, negative emotions about the course of economic events—anger or disgust— can make them downgrade the president's performance, perhaps against their better judgment. Furthermore, on the basis of the beta weights, these affective evaluations of the economy would even appear to have a somewhat greater impact on the electorate than the cognitive evaluations.

Still, such conclusions are far from definitive. For one, as Conover and Feldman (1986) recognize, the difficult problem of sorting out the causal linkages between the affective and cognitive evaluations persists. For another, these results are from a single community telephone survey, which did not ask respondents directly about vote intentions. Nevertheless, the work is intriguing enough to be developed further. Thus, in the special 1983 and 1984 Euro-Barometers, the following, admittedly exploratory, affective item was included:

> Do you ever feel angry about the way the present government is handling the economy? (never, seldom, sometimes, often, always).

The Euro-Barometer Surveys

The sometimes difficult local conditions for survey research on elections make the biannual Euro-Barometer public opinion surveys of the European Community an especially valuable social science resource. Begun in 1973, these surveys are conducted in every member nation. With these data a good deal of comparative research has been brought forward, the most well known being that of Inglehart (1977) on changing values in Western mass publics. These national surveys typically contain a variety of questions on social, cultural, and political topics, along with a standard set of demographic items, and are easily accessed by the scholarly community through the Inter-University Consortium for Political and Social Research (ICPSR) at the University of Michigan.

Nevertheless, they have been of little use to researchers interested in economic voting because of the tiny, changing pool of economic items that were asked (one past attempt with the available items was Lewis-Beck 1983). However, the National Science Foundation recently funded a battery of economic items to supplement the October, 1983, and April, 1984, Euro-Barometers (Nos. 20 and 21) in the five largest nations—Britain, France, Germany, Italy, and Spain.[2] These items, some already mentioned, tap the theoretical dimensions developed above—personal or collective, retrospective or prospective, simple or complex, cognitive or affective—and are fully presented in table 3.1.

Let us consider in more detail what the responses to these items say about economic conditions in these European nations. Earlier, we reviewed aggregate indicators of the economic problems they face. Now, with the surveys in hand, we can see these economic concerns manifest in citizen perceptions. In table 3.2 the distributions for central economic variables in the 1984 Euro-Barometer (No. 21) are presented. (Results from the earlier Euro-Barometer No. 20 are parallel.) Consider first the distribution of the family financial situation variable, which has been so much studied in United States surveys (see table 3.2A). In each of the five countries there are individuals who perceive their financial circumstances to have improved in comparison to the last year. However, the perception of financial deterioration is a more likely response. The picture is bleakest in France, where 53 percent of the sample saw their households as at least somewhat worse off, contrasted to only 8 percent who say things were at least somewhat better. The brightest outlook is West Germany, where just 23 percent perceived a worsening of personal finances, while the rest said they were the same (63 percent) or better (15 percent).

These variations in the perception of personal economic circumstances repeat themselves at the level of national economic perception (see table 3.2B), where a negative performance evaluation is more likely than a positive one. France is again at one pole, with fully 67 percent of the respondents declaring the country's economy had worsened over the past year. But Italy and Spain are not far behind, with scores of 59 percent and 54 percent, respectively. At the opposite pole once more is West Germany, where "worse" evaluations of the economy (26 percent) were actually balanced by "better" evaluations (26 percent).

These simple distributions reveal variation in economic perceptions, both

**TABLE 3.1   Economic Items in Euro-Barometers Nos. 20 and 21,
for Britain, France, Germany, Italy, Spain**

Personal

Simple retrospective
1. How does the financial situation of your household now compare with what it was 12 months ago? (lot better, better, same, little worse, lot worse)—personal finances.
2. Do you think that, over the last year, the income of your household has gone up more than the cost of living, has it fallen behind, or has it stayed about even with the cost of living? (gone up, stayed even, fallen behind)—real income.
3. As compared to a year ago, are people like yourself better off, worse off, or about the same financially? (better, same, worse)—peer finances.

Complex retrospective
1. Compared with a year ago, would you say that the government's policies have had a good effect, a bad effect, or that they really have not made much difference with regard to the financial situation of your household? (good, not much difference, bad)—government on self.
2. Compared to a year ago, would you say that the government's policies have had a good effect, a bad effect, or that they really have not made much difference with regard to the prospects of your keeping (or getting) a job? (good, not much difference, bad)—government on job.

Collective

Simple retrospective
1. How do you think the general economic situation in this country has changed over the last 12 months? (lot better, better, same, little worse, lot worse)—national economy.

Complex retrospective
1. Compared with a year ago, would you say that the government's policies have had a good effect, a bad effect, or that they really have not made much difference with regard to the country's general economic situation? (good, not much difference, bad)—government on economy.
2. Compared with a year ago, would you say that the government's policies have had a good effect, a bad effect, or that they really have not made much difference with regard to the unemployment issues? (good, not much difference, bad)—government on unemployment.
3. Compared with a year ago, would you say that the government's policies have had a good effect, a bad effect, or that they really have not made much difference with regard to prices? (good, not much difference, bad)—government on prices.

Complex retrospective affective
1. Do you ever feel angry about the way the present government is handling the economy? (never, seldom, sometimes, often, always)—anger.

Complex prospective
1. Do you think that, a year from now, the government's policies will have improved the country's general economic situation, will have made it worse, or that they will have not made much difference one way or another? (improved, not made much difference, made worse)—future policies.

Note: For clarity, the categories of response are given in parentheses, followed by a shorthand label for the item, as used in later tables.

within and across natons. According to economic voting notions, these differences should correspond to differences in political evaluations. Looking across
nations, one expectation is that government policy will be more critically
evaluated as the citizenry holds more negative views on economic conditions.
With these countries, economic perceptions (personal and collective) are most
pessimistic in France, most optimistic in Germany. Between these extremes
fall Spain, Italy, and Britain, in order. (The combined percentages of "lot
worse" and "little worse" on the personal finances and national economy
items—a sort of *perceptual misery index*—are as follows: France, 120; Spain,
98; Italy, 87; Britain, 73; Germany, 49.) Does aggregate public opinion on

TABLE 3.2   Frequency Distributions of Key Economic Items, 1984

	Britain	France	Germany	Italy	Spain
A. Personal Finances					
Lot worse	14%	17%	4%	6%	13%
Little worse	18	36	19	22	31
Same	43	39	63	57	44
Little better	19	6	13	13	10
Lot better	5	2	2	1	1
	100%	100%	100%	100%	100%
N	958	981	1,041	1,025	994
B. National Economy					
Lot worse	17%	30%	5%	21%	17%
Little worse	24	37	21	38	37
Same	28	28	47	22	29
Little better	28	6	24	18	16
Lot better	3	0	2	1	1
	100%	100%	100%	100%	100%
N	936	973	1,020	1,013	960
C. Government Effect on Economy					
Bad	34%	39%	28%	39%	41%
No difference	43	54	40	44	39
Good	23	8	33	17	19
	100%	100%	100%	100%	100%
N	939	924	951	967	886

Source: Euro-Barometer No. 21.

Note: For the full question and codes, see table 3.1. The columns of percentages
may not sum exactly to 100% because of rounding.

government policy in these countries correspond, in fact, to the ranking on this index?

To help answer this question, look at the third variable, in table 3.2C, which taps whether government policies have had a "good" effect, a "bad" effect, or "no" effect on the economy. One observes that the French are much more likely than the others to be dissatisfied with government economic policy. Indeed, 39 percent said the effect was "bad," as opposed to only 8 percent who said it was "good," for a percentage difference of +31. In Germany, still at the other end, the public was more likely to say that the policy effect of government was "good" (33 percent) rather than "bad" (28 percent), for a difference score of −5. Within this range, the other nations also line up about as before. Spain and Italy have a large share of citizens who are dissatisfied with government policy (41 percent and 39 percent, respectively), generating a difference score of +22 for each. Again, Britain is closest to the German end of the spectrum, with a difference of +11.

These national data comparisons, then, support the hypothesis that more public perception of economic deterioration (as measured by the so-called misery index) *is accompanied by more dissatisfaction with government action* (as measured by the "bad-good" percentage difference scores from table 3.2C). Is such dissatisfaction translated into votes against government? To begin a response, it is necessary to move from the above aggregated analysis, to individuals and their voting preferences.

Economic Voting: A Pass at the European Surveys

For the United States, the vote in national elections usually reduces to a choice between the two major parties. Thus, essential dimensions of difference can be collapsed into the simple Republican-Democrat dichotomy. With the multi-party systems of European democracies, however, various party arrays are possible. Perhaps the most common is an ordering along a Left-Right dimension. And historically, at least, a church-state schema has much to offer. Drawing on more recent experience, a system/antisystem party dichotomy has been proposed (Sartori 1966). Also, Lipset and Rokkan (1967) have suggested placing the parties on a territorial-cultural continuum. All these options rank the parties on a single, presumably overriding, dimension. Alternatively, rather than impose such order on the data, the analyst may prefer to view party selection as an attribute and treat it as a nominal variable (with all the statistical difficulties that implies).

Of course, the right decision depends on the purposes of the research. Here the aim is to test ideas about economic voting. In the American case, the basic assumption is that the citizen votes for (against) the incumbent if the incumbent provides more (less) economic benefits than the opposition. (But see Kiewiet 1981 on "policy-oriented" voting.) The logic is the same for multiparty systems. However, the incumbent is often a coalition of parties, rather than a single party as in the United States (see Downs 1957, chap. 9). The European economic voter, then, casts a ballot for or against a ruling coalition. (Assuming this is an entirely retrospective act, the traditional proposition on economic voting fully applies.) Therefore, the vote choice simplifies to an incumbency-opposition (1-0) dichotomy in the coding of responses to the Euro-Barometer vote intention item, "If there were a General Election tomorrow, which party would you support?"

Given the time period of the surveys, the following in-out dichotomies were thus constructed for the vote variable in these nations: Britain, the Conservatives versus the Labour, Liberal, Social Democrat, and Nationalist parties; France, the Socialist-led Left coalition versus the Gaullists, the UDF, and the small center and right parties; Germany, the Christian Democrats and Free Democrats versus the Social Democrats, Die Grünen, and smaller parties; Italy, the Socialists, Christian Democrats, Republicans, Liberals, and Social Democrats versus the Communists; Spain, the Socialists versus the Popular Alliance, the center parties, the Communists, and the regional parties.

How do economic conditions relate to this vote choice? It is conceivable that no relationship exists, because of the multiparty organization (Downs 1957, 143–45, 155–56). When the citizens of these nations indicate their votes, the election is for a legislature, which in turn has responsibility for selecting the government. Thus, these European voters cannot take such direct aim at the incumbent as, say, an American voter can in a presidential election. Further, while the economic policies of particular parties might be specific, the economic policies of party coalitions tend to be diffuse. Hence, the economic policies of the ruling coalition might be too vague, or at least too vaguely perceived, to provoke an electoral response. As a start, then, let us peek at some pivotal bivariate tables.

Recalling the cross-national analysis above, France and Germany represented the extremes of variation in economic perceptions (see table 3.2). Thus, they serve as convenient markers. Table 3.3A is a cross-tabulation of the personal finances variable with the recoded, dichotomous vote choice variable for France and Germany in the 1984 survey. The data support the pocketbook voter hypothesis, for those who perceive themselves to be financially worse off clearly have a higher probability of indicating a vote for an opposition party. More particularly, in the two countries, those who believe their personal economic circumstances have worsened are about twice as likely to express opposition support, when compared to those who feel economically better off.

These divisions are still sharper when variables on collective economic perceptions are examined. Look, for example, at the relationship between evaluation of government economic policy and vote choice in table 3.3B. The percentage differences are striking. For France, 79 percent of those who said government policy had "good" economic effects intended to vote for the ruling coalition, contrasted to only 30 percent of those who saw "bad" effects. With Germany, the respective percentages are similar, 83 percent versus 23 percent. These dramatic percentage differences—49 and 60—hint that the electorate's collective economic assessments have a good deal to do with vote choice in these countries. Of course, they are no more than a hint. We need to go on to examine other variables and countries as well.

TABLE 3.3   Cross-Tabulations of Vote Intention by Selected Personal and Collective Economic Perceptions, France and Germany, 1984

	A. Personal Finances			
	Lot Worse	Little Worse	Same	Little or Lot Better[a]
France (N = 768)				
Opposition	71%	55%	43%	41%
Incumbent	29	45	57	59
	100%	100%	100%	100%
Germany (N = 835)				
Opposition	80	67	50	39
Incumbent	20	33	50	61
	100%	100%	100%	100%

	B. Government Effect on Economy		
	Bad	No Difference	Good
France (N = 748)			
Opposition	70%	45%	21%
Incumbent	30	55	79
	100%	100%	100%
Germany (N = 807)			
Opposition	77	66	17
Incumbent	23	34	83
	100%	100%	100%

Source: Euro-Barometer No. 21.

Note: the full economic survey items and codes are given in table 3.1. "Opposition" refers to expression of a vote for a party in opposition, "incumbent" refers to expression of a vote for a party in the ruling coalition. The details of the coding of the dichotomous vote intention variable are given in table 3.4.

[a]The categories "little" and "lot better" are presented as one because of the scarcity of entries in the "lot better" category.

Useful preliminary tests come from correlating the vote choice variable in each country with all the economic variables (as measured by the survey items in table 4.1). If these bivariate relationships turn out to be generally feeble, then there is probably not much economic voting going on. (The possibility of suppressor effects would of course remain, but that alone offers negligible encouragement.) In table 3.4 the correlations (*r*) are reported for both the 1983 and 1984 Euro-Barometer surveys in the five nations. The associations are all in the expected direction, virtually all statistically significant (.05), and mostly moderate to strong across nations, items, and time.

TABLE 3.4   The Correlations (*r*) of the Economic Items with Vote Intention in Britain, France, Germany, Italy, and Spain, 1983–84

	Britain	France	Germany	Italy	Spain
Personal					
Simple retrospective					
Personal finances	.30 (.22)	.24 (.19)	.16 (.18)	.08' (.05')	.23 (.12)
Real income	.27 (.25)	.21 (.18)	.16 (.17)	.06' (.10)	.13 (.08)
Peer finances	.30 (.31)	.22 (.12)	.17 (.17)	.11 (.11)	.12 (.18)
Complex retrospective					
Government on self	.45 (.40)	.14 (.21)	.31 (.27)	.10 (.09)	.24 (.19)
Government on job	.37 (.46)	.35 (.12)	.35 (.33)	.13 (.11)	.23 (.14)
Collective					
Simple retrospective					
National economy	.48 (.52)	.43 (.38)	.38 (.38)	.12 (.22)	.35 (.31)
Complex retrospective					
Government on economy	.61 (.60)	.46 (.30)	.50 (.48)	.11 (.23)	.40 (.30)
Government on unemployment	.38 (.47)	.35 (.20)	.32 (.41)	.18 (.14)	.25 (.26)
Government on prices	.46 (.42)	.29 (.24)	.35 (.32)	.08 (.10)	.12 (.15)
Complex retrospective affective					
Anger	.56 (.51)	.41 (.36)	.47 (.38)	.14 (.20)	.31 (.28)
Complex prospective					
Future policies	.62 (.63)	.48 (.44)	.51 (.48)	.20 (.24)	.39 (.35)

Note: Coefficients without parentheses are from the 1983 survey, Euro-Barometer No. 20, and those in parentheses are from the 1984 survey, Euro-Barometer No. 21. All the coefficients achieve statistical significance at .05 or better, two-tail, except for the three denoted with an apostrophe ('). The dichotomous (1-0) vote intention variable codes the responses as follows for each country: Britain, 1 = Conservative, 0 = Labour, Social Democrat, Liberal, Nationalist; France, 1 = Socialist, Communist, MRG, PSU, 0 = RPR, Radical UDF, CDS/UDF, PR/UDF, Ecologist, National Front; Germany, 1 = CDU/CSU, FDP, 0 = SPD, NPD, DKP, Die Grünen; Italy, 1 = PSI, DC, PSDI, PRI, PLI, 0 = Communist; Spain, 1 = PSOE, 0 = AP, PDL, CDS, PCE, regional parties.

Summary and Conclusions

Economic voting appears commonplace, at least in American elections. How-ever, it is not, in the main, narrow pocketbook voting. Rather, it is more likely based on past assessments, both simple and complex, of national economic performance. It may also contain significant prospective and affective compo-nents, although this is not yet certain. A complete understanding of economic voting requires careful attention to all the dimensions—self to society, retro-spective to prospective, simple to complex, cognitive to affective. This re-quirement is meant to apply to Western Europe as well as the United States, although research on the former has only just begun. The next several chapters are devoted to unraveling the yarn of economic voting in the special Euro-Barometer surveys.

NOTES

1. The question of bias from item proximity, or "context effects," is profound for survey researchers of economics and politics. My research (1985b and unpublished) consistently finds that the proximity of relevant economic and political items in the NES surveys has no significant relationship to estimates of economic voting strength (or its lack). The particular economic item referred to is the standard one on personal finances, while the political items include presidential vote report, presidential vote intention, and presidential job approval. For those using these surveys to study economic voting, this is reassuring news.

   However, this does not mean that artifacts from item placement are every-where impossible. Sears and Lau (1983) provide convincing evidence that bias can be induced in an extreme, experimental situation. Specifically, when economic performance is the explicit subject of both the independent and dependent survey items and they are repeated in immediate proximity to each other, their correlation may be artifactually inflated. Further, such artifacts can be induced in certain kinds of nonexperimental survey situations, such as exit polls. Here, evidence comparing the Michigan election surveys (1976 and 1980) to the *CBS/New York Times* election exit polls (same years) seems definitive (Sears and Lau 1983, 237–42). Finally, with regard to the NES studies themselves, context effects have occurred with non-economic items. According to Bishop, Oldendick, and Tuchfarber (1984), NES respondents' judgments on their political interest level are influenced by whether the item is prefaced with hard questions about the representative's performance.

2. These 1983–84 survey data on economic conditions and attitudes in Britain, France, Germany, Italy, and Spain were gathered under United States National Science Foundation Grant SES 83-06020 (awarded to the author) as a subcontract to the Euro-Barometer organization of the European Community. The specific Euro-Barometers involved were No. 20 (October–November, 1983) and No. 21 (March–April, 1984), directed by Jacques-René Rabier with Ronald Inglehart. The field

work for the surveys was coordinated out of the offices of Faits et Opinions, headed by Hélène Riffault in Paris. The interviews were carried out by the following local polling firms: Britain, Social Surveys (Gallup Poll); France, Institut de Sondages Lavialle; Germany, EMNID; Italy, Istituto Doxa; Spain, Emopublica. The Euro-Barometers always aim for national samples of 1,000. For example, here are the specific total sample sizes for Euro-Barometer No. 21: Britain, 1,042; France, 1,008; Germany, 992; Italy, 1,060; Spain, 1,016. These data are available through the Inter-University Consortium for Political and Social Research (University of Michigan) to its members. It goes without saying that none of these institutions, American or European, bears any responsibility for the analysis and conclusions herein.

Part 2 Western Europe: A Cross-national Perspective

Voter

self   society

affective   cognitive

retrospective   prospective

simple   complex

considering everything

Chapter 4

The European Voter:
Economics, Cleavages, Ideology

> The Socialists stormed back into power in France in 1981, figuring they could turn the country around by stimulating the economy. They increased the minimum wage, boosted old-age pensions, added to the civil-service job rolls—and failed miserably. (*Wall Street Journal,* June 17, 1985, 22)

> "Pockets?" said Corduroy to himself. "I don't have a pocket!" (Don Freeman, *A Pocket for Corduroy* [Cedar Grove, N.J.: Puffin Books, Rae Publishing, 1978])

Imagine a European voter, M. Jean Q. Citizen, whose decision to vote for or against the incumbent is motivated entirely by economic considerations. How might this decision work? The foregoing discussion of theory and evidence suggests he will rely on retrospective and prospective economic evaluations of self and society. Further, these evaluations may be affective as well as cognitive, complex as well as simple. That is, he regards the past and the future, focusing on his own economic circumstances and those of the nation. At the center of his evaluation is the role of government, to which he does not always react dispassionately. Overall, as any of these assessments become negative, M. Citizen is more likely to vote against the incumbent. Further, all these assessments, taken together, totally determine his vote.

Unfortunately, we cannot measure the myriad of such economic considerations, large and small, which guide European voters. But central ones have been calibrated in the special Euro-Barometers (see table 3.1), and with these considerations in mind, this idealized voting scenario becomes somewhat more concrete. Prior to the ballot, Jean contemplates how his family has been faring financially (personal simple retrospective evaluation = X_1). He also regards the performance of the national economy (collective simple retrospective evaluation = X_2). While viewing these economic conditions, he judges the impact of government. Has government action made my private economic circumstances better or worse (personal complex retrospective evaluation = X_3)? Have government policies helped improve the country's business picture (collective complex retrospective evaluation = X_4)? Further, he considers what these policies are likely to bring in the future (collective complex prospective evaluation = X_5). Lastly, these evaluations have some emotional content, reducing to anger or joy over how things are going (collective complex retrospective affective evaluation = X_6). Assuming these variables exhaust the dimensions of economic evaluation, the vote of M. Jean Q. Citizen is determined as follows:

$$V = f(X_1, X_2, X_3, X_4, X_5, X_6) \tag{4.1}$$

where V = vote intention, a dichotomous incumbent-opposition choice measured as in table 3.4; X_1–X_6 are economic evaluation variables, labeled in table 3.1 as follows: X_1 = personal finances, X_2 = national economy, X_3 = government on self, X_4 = government on economy, X_5 = future policies, X_6 = anger.

Estimates for an Ideal Economic Voter Model

This pure economic voter model is estimated in table 4.1. The results strongly support the presence of economic voting in these five electorates. In general, the coefficients are in the expected direction. That is, the worse the economic condition is perceived, the greater the individual preference for an opposition party. Further, these coefficients are mostly significant at .05 or better. Also, the goodness-of-fit statistics favor a vigorous economic interpretation of the

TABLE 4.1   Ideal Economic Voting Equation (OLS), by Nation, 1984

	Britain	France	Germany	Italy	Spain
Personal finances (X_1)	−.03	.00	−.02	−.03	−.04
National economy (X_2)	.06***	.11***	.04**	.07**	.08***
Government on self (X_3)	.07***	−.03	.04	.00	.08**
Government on economy (X_4)	.14***	.03	.16***	.07**	.04
Future policies (X_5)	.19***	.21***	.18***	.07**	.14***
Anger (X_6)	.08***	.08***	.09***	.05***	.07***
Constant	−.71***	−.40***	−.63***	.24***	.95***
R^2	.53	.28	.34	.11	.23
N	711	642	734	522	479

*$p < .10$, **$p < .05$, ***$p < .01$, in the expected direction.
Source: Euro-Barometer No. 21.
Codes: For the vote variable, see table 3.4; for personal finances and national economy, lot better = 5, better = 4, same = 3, little worse = 2, worse = 1; government on self and government on economy, good = 3, not much difference = 2, bad = 1; future policies, improved = 3, not made much difference = 2, made worse = 1; anger, never = 5, seldom = 4, sometimes = 3, often = 2, always = 1.

vote choice in these Western European nations, especially for Britain, with R^2 = .53. Overall, then, within the constraints of a strictly economic model, the findings are pleasing statistically. Moreover, the model has some theoretical appeal, for it exhausts the more global indicators of the relevant evaluation dimensions, and various experiments with index construction yielded no improvement on this count.

These estimates, admittedly preliminary and based on idealized notions of party choice, hint that economics shapes the Western European voter. Still, all economic variables do not sweep the field. What fails to achieve conventional statistical significance in every country is the variable of personal finances. The evidence just does not support the pocketbook voter argument.

evidence doesn't support pocketbook voting in Western Europe

This conclusion is strengthened by measurement considerations. Recall that the personal finances item parallels the Michigan item on family financial situation, except that it is five-category rather than three-category. On the basis of the work by Rosenstone and his colleagues (1983) discussed earlier, this expansion of categories should yield better item performance. Nevertheless, once other economic factors are taken into account, it still engenders no relationship with vote. Furthermore, other possible measures of individual economic circumstance, which are perhaps less "noisy" than X_1, do not enhance the case for pocketbook voting. Specifically, when the other available personal simple retrospective items—"real income" and "peer finances"— are substituted for this standard "personal finances" item, the lack of support for the hypothesis continues.

further support this notion

In each of these nations, whether voters are doing better or worse financially seems to have virtually no effect on party preference in these legislative contests. Indeed, the summary is quite similar to that on U.S. congressional election survey evidence: *For legislative elections in these Western European countries, simple pocketbook evaluations have a negligible impact on individual vote choice.*

also no effect on party preference

Pocketbook voting, then, at least in any direct or obvious sense, is absent. However, personal finances perhaps play a subtle, more contingent role in the voter calculus. Certainly, this is the implication of the coefficients of the "government on self" variable (X_3), which are sometimes significant in table 4.1. But these suggestive coefficients may be biased upward. Indeed, most of the coefficients in these naive, economically driven models have to be biased, because of omitted explanatory variables. Therefore, prior to considering the impact of these particular kinds of economic evaluations, it is necessary to specify more properly the vote equation.

Rival Explanations of the Western European Voter

In studies of Western European electorates, the economic voter perspective is relatively untried. Instead, what dominates is an emphasis on social cleavages or, to a lesser extent, on partisanship. The former tradition is the more venerable of the two. The social cleavages approach attempts to explain voter preferences from structural differences in society, especially those of class and religion. (Classics in this tradition include Alford 1963; Lijphart 1971; Lipset 1960; Lipset and Rokkan 1967; Rose and Urwin 1969.) With regard to social class, the persistent finding is that workers (blue-collar occupations) are more likely than the bourgeoisie (white-collar occupations) to vote for parties on the Left. Recently, a good deal of attention has been given to the possible decline of such class-based voting (see Inglehart 1984). Nevertheless, it still continues in the nations under study, although perhaps diminished. (Elsewhere, I have argued that, at least in France, class voting shows no signs of decline; Lewis-Beck 1981, 1984a.) The second key cleavage variable is religion. In study after study, those who are more faithful in their religious practices are shown to be more supportive of Center and Right parties. For countries like Italy, this relationship is especially strong. Indeed, the overall conclusion of Rose and Urwin (1969, 12) would still seem to hold: ". . . religious divisions, not class, are the main social basis of parties in the Western world today."

An alternative to a social cleavages explanation of the vote is one emphasizing partisanship. The core idea is familiar: the voter has a long-term, psychological attachment to a partisan object, which directs political preferences. The paradigm here is the party identification concept developed from the Michigan election studies (Campbell et al. 1960). The survey item used to measure the concept reads as follows: "Do you consider yourself a Democrat, a Republican, an Independent, or what?" Efforts to apply such a measure and concept of party identification to Western European electorates have met with mixed success (Dalton, Beck, and Flanagan 1984, 11–15; Budge, Crewe, and Fairlie 1976). Apparently, when administered to European voters, such items are routinely taken to be direct questions about vote intention, rather than party attachment. Thus, party and vote items are intertwined, exhibiting almost no statistical independence. Moreover, if more exploratory, open-ended items are used, party identification rates appear very low, perhaps artifactually. (The French case provides a telling example; see Lewis-Beck 1984.)

Given these problems with a standard party identification approach to the vote in Western Europe, must we abandon the notion that long-term, partisan attachments drive these electorates? No. A growing body of research suggests that in the multiparty systems of Western Europe the enduring commitment is to an ideology, rather than a party. A voter's ideology is conceived of as a psychological anchor on a Left-to-Right dimension. (The use of ideology in this context should not be confused with its other meaning, as a "belief-system constraint"; see Converse 1964.) European surveys have long asked interviewees to relate themselves to a Left-Right political spectrum. Indeed, in France the major polling organization, IFOP, was reporting frequency dis-

What happens when a party strays from their typical ideological position? Polarization?

tributions on Left-Right items as far back as 1946. Western Europeans, unlike Americans, have easily placed themselves on such a continuum, as the typically small percentage of nonresponses suggests.

The Euro-Barometer, in particular, always asks this question: "In political matters people talk of the Left and the Right. How would you place your views on the scale?" (The respondent is shown a ten-point scale going from "Left" to "Right.") Inglehart and Klingemann (1976, 269) have extensively explored the partisan character of this ideology item, concluding that "Left-right self-placement corresponds very closely to political party identification everywhere except in Ireland." Other researchers have even suggested that, for those Western European systems with many parties, *ideological identification* is the preferred conceptualization of long-term partisanship (Lancaster and Lewis-Beck 1986; Lewis-Beck 1983; Percheron and Jennings 1981). In their careful study on the Netherlands, a critical test case, van der Eijk and Niemoller (1983) found that this ideological identification was quite stable over time. (In contrast, responses to standard party identification questions were very unstable, with 49 percent of voters changing their party identification once or more over a five-month period.) Further, "parties constitute real world entities which allow a person to approximately express his own ideological position" (van der Eijk and Niemoller 1983, 28). *That is, these voters do have, following V. O. Key, a "standing decision" that orients their political choices, but it is a commitment to ideology rather than party.*

Inglehart: ideology corresponds w/ partyID very well ↓ except in Ireland?

Three distinct approaches to understanding voters in the leading Western European nations have been proposed—*economic voting, social cleavages, and partisan identification* (cf. Powell's [1983] valuable essay). These explanations are not really "rival," in that it is not necessary to choose among them. Nevertheless, in practice, researchers seem to do precisely that, pursuing one approach and ignoring the others. The current wave of economic voting research seems no exception, but rather is "a theme which has taken on a life of its own as a focus of comparative voting behavior studies" (Powell 1983, 34). The ideal economic voter model estimated in table 4.1 obviously perpetuates this exclusivity. Clearly, an amalgamation of these approaches, the old and the new, is needed. This will allow a more complete explanation of the vote choice and, at the same time, afford a more accurate assessment of the relative effects of the competing sets of variables.

Therefore, to improve the model, I incorporated central social cleavage and partisanship variables, i.e., social class, religion, and ideological identification. As expected, these variables correlate well with vote intention. (For instance, here are bivariate correlations [r] with vote intention of class, religion, and ideology, respectively, from Euro-Barometer No. 20: France, .20, .24, .70; Britain, .22, .10, .49; Germany, .15, .21, .61; Italy, .26, .34, .62.) The measures employed are the usual ones, as follows: social class (blue-collar

included cleavages + partisanship variables

class, religion, ideology

versus non-blue-collar occupations for head of household); religion (degree to which respondents consider themselves religious practitioners); ideological identification (self-placement on the ten-point Left-Right scale). Conceptually, then, the revised model becomes

$$\text{Vote} = f(\text{Economics, Cleavages, Ideology}) \qquad (4.2)$$

where Vote = intention to vote for an incumbent or an opposition party, Economics = the significant economic forces identified in eq. 4.1; Cleavages = social class and religion; ideology = self-identification along a Left-Right continuum.

In terms of the specific variables, the equation to be estimated expresses itself as follows:

$$V = a_1 + b_2X_2 + b_3X_3 + b_4X_4 + b_5X_5 + b_6X_6 + c_1Z_1 + c_2Z_2$$

$$+ c_3Z_3 + e \qquad (4.3)$$

where V = vote intention, 1 = incumbent party, 0 = opposition party; $X_2 - X_6$ are economic variables, again measured and labeled as in eq. 4.1; Z_1 = social class, 1 = working-class occupation for head of household, 0 = middle-class occupation for head of household; Z_2 = religiosity, where 1 = religious

TABLE 4.2   Full Single-Equation Voting Model (OLS), by Nation, 1983

	Britain	France	Germany	Italy
National economy (X_2)	.003	.03*	−.007	.01
Government on self (X_3)	.05**	.03	.006	−.01
Government on economy (X_4)	.12***	.03	.09***	.03
Future policies (X_5)	.21***	.05*	.10***	.06**
Anger (X_6)	.08***	.04**	.09***	.03*
Social class (Z_1)	−.05*	.10***	−.11***	−.16***
Religiosity (Z_2)	.02	.03	−.04	−.12***
Ideological ID (Z_3)	.04***	−.12***	.10***	.12***
Constant	−.74***	.63***	−.64***	.15*
R^2	.54	.53	.48	.48
N	475	427	435	355

*$p < .10$, **$p < .05$, ***$p < .01$, in the expected direction.

Source: Euro-Barometer No. 20.

Codes: The vote and the economic variables are coded as in table 4.1; social class = occupation of head of household, 0 = middle, 1 = working; religiosity, 1 = religious person, 2 = not a religious person, 3 = atheist; ideological identification, a 1–10 self-placement scale from Left to Right.

person, 2 = not a religious person, 3 = atheist; Z_3 = ideological identification, measured on a 1–10 Left-Right self-placement scale, all as measured in Euro-Barometer No. 20.

The parameter estimates (OLS) appear in table 4.2.[1] Further, because of possible concerns over the dichotomous nature of the dependent variable, the logit estimates appear in table 4.3. These more fully specified results shed light on several questions. *What about the impact of economic evaluations? Do they hold up, when pitted against the established forces of class, religion, and ideology? The unqualified answer is yes, as a glance at the significance tests suggests.*

Before considering the matter further, we ought to prepare ourselves with an assessment of the general goodness of the model in a statistical sense. The "pseudo-R" of the logit models all fall around .70, which is encouraging. Unfortunately, fit statistics for such models have not been completely de-bugged (Aldrich and Nelson 1986; Berry and Lewis-Beck 1986, 113). There-fore, it is useful to look as well at the regressions R^2, each around a healthy .5. A worry with the R^2, though, is its sensitivity to variance changes in the independent variables from sample to sample (Achen 1982; Lewis-Beck and Skalaban 1988). It is reassuring to observe that an alternative summary statis-tic, the standard error of estimate, gives quite stable cross-sample predictions for each country. In table 4.4, the equation is replicated for the later samples in Euro-Barometer No. 21.[2] These stable standard errors of estimate are as

TABLE 4.3 Full Single-Equation Voting Model (Logit), by Nation, 1983

	Britain	France	Germany	Italy
National economy (X_2)	0.06	0.24**	0.03	0.20*
Government on self (X_3)	0.43***	0.20	0.28*	−0.39
Government on economy (X_4)	0.73***	0.24	0.44***	0.32*
Future policies (X_5)	1.56***	0.31*	0.75***	0.52***
Anger (X_6)	0.65***	0.33***	0.75***	0.17*
Social class (Z_1)	−.46***	0.81***	−0.70***	−1.41***
Religiosity (Z_2)	0.17	0.16	−0.30**	−0.66***
Ideological ID (Z_3)	0.42***	−0.99***	0.79***	1.14***
Constant	−10.14***	1.16*	−9.10***	−3.55***
Pseudo-R	.71	.70	.66	.70
Weighted *N*	941	741	997	698

*$p < .10$, **$p < .05$, ***$p < .01$, in the expected direction.

Source: Euro-Barometer No. 20.

Codes: The same as in table 4.2. The logit estimates were carried out with SAS. The concept of a "pseudo-R" is similar but not identical to the OLS counterpart, a multiple R. Notice that these pseudo-R, if squared, would approximate the OLS R^2 values.

**TABLE 4.4 Full Single-Equation Voting Model (OLS), All
Nations, 1984**

	Britain	France	Germany	Italy	Spain
National economy (X_2)	.03*	.01	.03	.04**	.04**
Government on self (X_3)	.04*	.00	.03	.01	.03
Government on economy (X_4)	.14***	.00	.11***	.07***	.05*
Future policies (X_5)	.13***	.06*	.12***	.03	.11***
Anger (X_6)	.08***	.04*	.04*	.02	.06***
Social class (Z_1)	−.09***	.04	−.01	−.17***	.07***
Religiosity (Z_2)	.00	.00	.03**	.09***	.003
Ideological ID (Z_3)	.06***	−.15***	.10***	.08***	−.06***
Constant	−.80***	.97***	−.89***	−.33***	.95***
R^2	.56	.53	.48	.39	.31
N	454	411	435	332	400

*$p < .10$, **$p < .05$, ***$p < .01$, in the expected direction.

Source: Euro-Barometer No. 21.

Codes: The variables are coded as in table 4.3, with a few exceptions because of different item availability across surveys. Except for Spain, religiosity is here measured with a five-point agree-disagree scale on the existence of God; for Spain, religiosity is measured with six-point frequency of religious practice scale, from "never" to "several times per week." Also for Spain, social class is measured with a subjective four-point self-placement scale from "upper" to "lower."

follows, for the 1983 and 1984 surveys, respectively: France, .46 and .46; Britain, .55 and .56; Germany, .55 and .56; Italy, .47 and .50; Spain, .41. Overall, then, this single-equation model seems a secure base for serious consideration of economic effects on the Western European voter.

Another Look at Pocketbook Voting

Do changing perceptions of economic conditions by these electorates influence the vote? Not each and every one. In particular, the complex pocketbook voting effects suggested earlier fail to sustain themselves. The variable, "government on self" (X_3), generally fails to register statistical significance at conventional levels. *The fact that European citizens may attribute to government a "good" or a "bad" effect on their pocketbooks does not appear, in itself, to have an influence on parliamentary vote intention.*

    Let us consider this null finding more carefully. Among advocates of the pocketbook voter, a key criticism of the usually weak survey findings is inadequacy of measurement. Following Kramer (1983), a good deal of variance in "simple" personal economic well-being, (e.g., now you are "better off," now "worse off") would seem to have nothing to do with government policies. Therefore, these items are politically "noisy," and when related to the vote will produce feeble coefficients. By implication, what is needed are items that separate out the government- and non-government-induced components of financial variation. This Euro-Barometer item attempts to do so, explicitly asking respondents what kind of an "effect" government policies had on household finances. Nevertheless, this improved measurement nets no new, hitherto undiscovered, direct effects from the pocketbook. Why?

It is worth noting, first, that a fairly large proportion of these Western European publics believe that, for good or ill, government has influenced their personal financial situation. (Specifically, the percentages of respondents in 1984 who said their government had some effect on their finances are as follows: Britain, 45 percent; France, 44 percent; Germany, 40 percent; Italy, 34 percent; Spain, 49 percent.) These attitudes would seem to stand in marked contrast to the United States, where Kinder and Mebane (1983) found that the percentage of American respondents willing to attribute personal financial well-being to government never rose above 20 percent. Even taking into account the gross measurement differences, important cross-cultural variation would seem to be occurring here. Western Europeans are much more likely than Americans to assign influence over family finances to government (see the earlier work by Katona, Strumpels, and Zahn 1971).

Indeed, public acceptance of government influences over personal finances approaches a "norm" in Western Europe. As something of a norm, it is not especially remarkable. Acting alone, it cannot trigger a vote either for or against the responsible governing coalition. The voter thinks, "While government today may be adversely affecting my pocketbook, tomorrow things may be better." The key to a vote switch, then, ultimately depends on whether the citizen feels that the policies of the ruling coalition will bring a better day. In the end, it is such collective evaluations, rather than personal ones, that move European electorates.

The Effects of Collective Economic Voting

The collective items about government are what tap economic voting in Western Europe, according to the parameter estimates (shown in tables 4.2–4.4). In each country, a negative evaluation of national economic policies and programs substantially increases the chances of an anti-incumbent vote. The three variables tapping perceptions of national government economic performance—"government on economy" (X_4), "future policies" (X_5), "anger" (X_6)—almost always manage statistical significance, even after the extensive controls on each other and on the rival explanatory variables.[3] In table 4.5, the model is reestimated (logit) to reflect this more streamlined specification of economic effects.

These different evaluation dimensions are unified by one concern in the

voter's mind—Is the government doing a good job running the economy? A
yes answer clearly strengthens the intention to vote for a party in the ruling
coalition. In fact, the results would seem to allow the following preliminary
generalization: *For legislative elections in these Western European countries,
collective economic evaluations exercise, at the least, a moderate impact on
individual vote choice.*

This is a satisfying conclusion, compatible with reports from congressional elections in the U.S. case. Such cross-cultural validation has obvious
importance. For one, it bolsters confidence in a central notion underlying
economic voting theory; i.e., in a democratic polity (*any* democratic polity),
voters express their economic dissatisfactions at the ballot box. If this notion is
true, then it should be readily confirmed in surveys from a variety of democratic nations, as it is here. However, while this conclusion is comforting, it is
not especially surprising. After all, we are accustomed to supposing that
electorates punish incumbents for poor past performance. But what does
surprise are the significant findings on the affective and prospective components of economic voting.

Of all the economic variables in this single-equation model of the Western
European voter, none is statistically more secure than the prospective item
(X_5), which asks respondents to evaluate the economic effects of government
actions over the next year. Its coefficient is statistically significant at conventional levels in every country. Furthermore, that coefficient consistently attains
higher significance levels compared to the others. These Western Europeans
evidently judge how government and the economy will do and alter their vote

**TABLE 4.5   Reduced Single-Equation Voting Model (Logit), All
Nations, 1984**

	Britain	France	Germany	Italy	Spain
Government on economy (X_4)	1.21***	0.18[a]	0.61***	0.83***	0.33**
Future policies (X_5)	1.15***	0.41**	1.08***	0.40**	0.65***
Anger (X_6)	0.91***	0.26**	0.36***	0.19*	0.28***
Social class (Z_1)	−0.83***	0.32*	−0.18	−1.55***	0.15
Religiosity (Z_2)	−0.01	0.01	0.25***	0.58***	0.008
Ideological ID (Z_3)	0.68***	−1.28***	0.76***	0.69***	−0.32***
Constant	−11.68***	4.43***	−9.69***	−6.17***	1.56**
Pseudo-R	.65	.72	.66	.62	.43
Weighted N	903	769	1,073	650	519

*$p < .10$, **$p < .05$, ***$p < .01$, in the expected direction.
Source: Euro-Barometer No. 21.
Codes: The variables are coded as in table 4.4.
[a]Significant at .22, in the expected direction.

intentions accordingly. When they perceive that government policies are likely to harm the economy over the next year, they withdraw support from the incumbent coalition.

Furthermore, this prospective evaluation does not appear to be merely a Downsian projection from retrospective economic performance, as some might argue. Instead, as the multivariate estimates demonstrate, the prospective variable has this consequential impact independently, *even after controlling for the various retrospective variables*. While a component of future expectations is undoubtedly shaped by past performance, prospective considerations still achieve considerable impact in their own right. The following cautious generalization would therefore seem appropriate: *For legislative elections in these Western European countries, collective economic prospective evaluations exercise, by themselves, a nontrivial impact on individual vote choice*.

Perhaps the most provocative of all the findings is that on affective economic voting. According to these estimates, feelings of anger over government economic performance translate into significant reductions in incumbent party support in each country studied. Moreover, these emotional reactions to government action manage to color the political responses of these publics, quite apart from the cognitive evaluations the voter may hold. That is, the voter's negative reaction to government economic policy does not spend itself in a formal, more or less rational criticism. Reacting to the economy, a European voter may, as Weatherford (1983, 161) puts it, process information in "the most logical and efficient way possible." But besides that, this voter might possess an "angry feeling" which, on its own, pushes him or her away from the incumbent.

Stated another way, there seems to be an affective dimension to political economic evaluation, as well as a cognitive dimension. This is a controversial stance and certainly cannot be regarded as well established on the basis of these initial tests, though some empirical support does come from the pilot work of Conover and Feldman (1986) in the United States. These results, taken together, encourage further research on the affective economic voter hypothesis, and they provide stimulation for more investigation of the whole psychological process that underlies economic voting. We still know relatively little about the mechanisms, cognitive or otherwise, behind these important economic judgments. Certainly, this is a fertile area for controlled experimental work, as well as additional survey research (for relevant efforts in social psychology, see Tetlock 1983; Tourangeau 1984; Tyler, Rasinski, and McGraw 1985).

Summary and Conclusions

This survey evidence offers a rather clear picture of the vote decision in Western European electorates. What tugs at Western European voters? First, there are long-term forces of a social and a psychological nature. As earlier scholarship has also demonstrated, traditional ties to class and religion reliably orient them. And as many scholars are coming to realize, attachment to an ideology, on the Left or Right, also acts as quite a powerful pointer for Western European voters. In addition to social cleavages and ideological identification, this research indicates that economic issues are important determinants of the individual vote choice in these five nations—Britain, France, Germany, Italy, and Spain. Economics motivates these voters in many, though not all, ways. They are not short-sighted opportunists who vote for or against government simply according to their pocketbooks. If they act on the basis of economic self-interest, the calculations must be embedded in a larger overall view of the fate of the collectivity. When government mishandling of the economy is perceived, individuals respond and ruling coalitions lose votes. Perhaps surprisingly, this punishment of the incumbent is based as much on prospective evaluations as on retrospective ones. Moreover, it appears not to be derived entirely from rational calculation, for passions such as "anger" over government policy operate independently of these other collective evaluations. Other questions about the economic voter in Western Europe remain. At this juncture, though, one thing seems clearly established: proper specification of voting models for Western European electorates demands that economic variables be given a prominent place.

NOTES

1. A full equation for Spain could not be estimated with the Euro-Barometer No. 20 data, because of measurement inadequacies on the noneconomic variables; however, Spain could be included in Euro-Barometer No. 21 estimations.
2. From all the nations, the OLS estimates for Britain appear the strongest. Therefore, it seems especially important to compare those results to estimates from a technique that takes explicit account of *all* the categorical properties of these data. Thus, here are the logit estimates (SAS) for the British equation (Euro-Barometer No. 21). The estimation procedure here is quite strict (and cumbersome), because an effort has been made to meet interval-level measurement assumptions for the right-hand side variables (witness the long string of dummy variables). As can be seen, the model fits the data well, and all the economic variables continue to exhibit a high level of statistical significance.

Dependent Variable = Vote Intention (0,1)

Independent Variables	Coefficient
government on economy (good)	0.87***
government on economy (bad)	−0.79**
future policies (improve)	1.07***
future policies (worse)	−1.16**

Independent Variables	Coefficient
national economy (better)	0.17
national economy (worse)	−1.00***
government on self (good)	0.99**
government on self (bad)	0.03
anger (seldom or never)	0.96***
anger (often or always)	−1.36***
ideology (left)	−1.24***
ideology (right)	0.74**
religiosity (low)	−1.43***
religiosity (medium)	−0.83**
social class	−0.55**
intercept	0.40

pseudo-R = .71
** $p < .05$, *** $p < .01$, in the expected direction.

The variables are the same as in table 4.4; however, here they are entered categorically in a series of dummies (always recognizing the G-1 restriction).

3. Interestingly, a standard collective variable (X_2) on the performance of the "national economy," in itself, sometimes exhibits no independent impact on the vote. While this finding may seem unexpected, its explanation is straightforward: the variable is largely redundant with the other collective economic variables ($X_3–X_5$). The most obvious redundancy is its relationship with "government on economy" (X_4). The correlation (r) of X_2 and X_4 surpasses .50 in each of these nations (except Italy, where it attains .37 in Euro-Barometer No. 21). Besides the statistical overlap of these variables, there is also a theoretical redundancy. While both ask about the national economy, one (X_2) seeks a "simple" evaluation without reference to government, the other (X_4) seeks a "complex" evaluation linking the two. Arguably, the second item contains the needed information in terms of economic voting theory, for it explicitly couples the economic assessment with government. This psychological step would seem logically necessary in order for economic voting actually to take place. Hence, the "simple" item adds no new information. Of course, this does not mean that "simple" evaluations of the national economy are irrelevant to partisan preferences. Rather, it implies that their path to these preferences is indirect. In particular, general evaluations of the national economy would be expected to contribute to specific evaluations of government economic performance (X_4).

Chapter 5

Noneconomic Issues, Class Interactions, Asymmetric Voters: Other Possibilities

> The fact that economic conditions influence voters is a leading commonplace of conversation in election years. The question is: Is this fact in fact a fact? (Stigler 1973, 160)

> The cornfields of the Midwest are so factual that they seem to discredit everything unempirical. (Suzannah Lessard, "A Reporter At Large, Transcontinental Journey," *New Yorker*, October 14, 1984, 55)

The model of Western European vote choice developed in chapter 4, while it may have appealing theoretical and statistical properties, is certainly not above challenge. Serious questions are yet to be settled. First, should additional independent variables be included? Surely issues besides economics motivate these electorates. If so, do these other issues diminish, even eliminate, the effects of economic conditions? Second, supposing economic effects are sustained, is the form of the relationship adequately specified? In particular, the impact of economic perceptions on party preference may actually be more interactive than additive, perhaps depending on social class. Or it might be that the influence of economic conditions is oddly asymmetric, with voters punishing incumbents for hard times but failing to reward them for good times. These questions—of noneconomic issues, interactions, and asymmetry—are considered below.

Issue Voting

Obviously, noneconomic issues can affect the Western European voter. The potential list is long—crime, workers' rights, government waste, pollution, student unrest, nuclear weapons, energy, abortion, immigration, and terrorism, among others. It might be argued that a model should take into account such issues, in order to explain fully the vote choice.[1] Further, and more worrisome, there is the prospect that once these variables are included, the reportedly strong economic effects will fade away. Indeed, there is some

69

suggestion that these more contemporary issues are crowding out the impact of traditional economic concerns (Dalton 1988, chap. 6).

The Western European model developed in chapter 4 obviously lacks overt measures on noneconomic issues. Nevertheless, the interpretation of the economic coefficients remains unproblematic to the extent that two conditions are met: (1) the ideological identification variable captures, indirectly, the effect of noneconomic issues; and (2) noneconomic issue variables, though not included, are uncorrelated with the included economic variables. When these conditions are met, the absence of explicit noneconomic issue variables on the right-hand side of the vote equation will not inflate the parameter estimates for the economic variables. Of course, to the extent that neither of these conditions hold, it is advisable to bring the other issue variables into the equation. This I do below, after first considering more carefully the role of ideological identification in the general model.

As mentioned earlier, the status of the ideology variable in Western European voting models is somewhat ambiguous, much like that of party identification in American voting models. The question boils down to this: "How endogenous is it?" At the one extreme, it is seen as wholly exogenous, a steady long-term psychological identification that directs voter preference from one election to the next. At the other extreme, it is seen as wholly endogenous, determined by short-term events and issues, fluctuating greatly from election to election. As it actually functions, the status of the ideology variable falls somewhere between these extremes.

Undeniably, there is an exogenous component to Left-Right ideological self-placement. Almost all Western Europeans can readily make such a self-placement, and such identification seems to be inherited, to some extent, from parents. Jennings (1984) and Percheron and Jennings (1981) have carefully examined the transmission of ideological orientation from parent to child in Western European publics, drawing for the most part on the Political Action national surveys in the 1970s (Barnes et al. 1979). In the nations under study here, they found the following correlations between parent-youth Left-Right self-placement: Britain, .31; France, .44; Germany, .20; Italy, .43. These moderate associations clearly suggest that some ideological attachment is exogenous, acquired by past parental socialization and applied to guide present choices.

But while part of the ideological identification variable is exogenous, it may only be a small part. Indeed, endogeneity may dominate (especially in Germany, where parent-child ideological transmission appears weakest). As in the United States research on party identification, the possibility of endogeneity is increasingly appreciated. Fiorina's (1981, chap. 5) idea of party identification as a weighted "running tally" of past performance nicely summarizes currents in this revisionist thinking. A parallel in the Western European case is the consideration of Left-Right ideology as a "superissue," an issue standing above and encompassing a host of lesser, more specific issues (see Dalton 1988, chap. 9). This view is captured well by Inglehart (1984, 37):

> The Left-Right dimension, as a political concept, is a higher-level abstraction used to summarize one's stand on the important political issues of the day. It serves the function of organizing and simplifying a complex political reality, providing an overall orientation . . . .

For example, a self-declared "leftist" is one who is for unions, immigrants, and ecology, and against nuclear energy, censorship, and military spending. Suppose, indeed, ideological self-placement captures, in one score, the voter's stance on a wide range of issues, then the earlier equations (see tables 4.2–5) are well-specified after all, for they include the "superissue" of ideology.

Overall, this argument is encouraging. Certainly, ideological identification is made up, at least in part, of immediate issue positions. Therefore, its presence in the vote equation does help control for the influence of noneconomic issues, reassuring us that economics does matter. Still, the orientation to Left and Right on the part of these Western electorates has been shown to have some life of its own, separate from specific events. Further, all issue stances surely cannot be neatly predicted from a single, common Left-Right scale. Given these circumstances, mere control on Left-Right ideology itself would seem insufficient. In order to establish firmly the magnitude of economic effects, it would be well to carry out an additional direct examination of measures on noneconomic issues.

Fortunately, Euro-Barometer No. 21 contains a large number of issue items, which permits an exploration of alternative specifications. In particular, twenty-two items measuring voter positions on a broad range of social, cultural, and policy issues were located. They touch on most, if not all, the important topics of the day: local government, neighborhood safety, quality of housing, public services, ecology, violence, workers' rights, censorship, energy, nuclear power, government intervention, homosexuality, inequality, race, immigrant workers, and European unification. (Many of these issues might be classified as "postmaterialist," in contrast to the economic issues which could be classified as "materialist" [Inglehart 1984].) What is the impact of these noneconomic issues on vote choice? Do they diminish the impact of economic issues? If so, how much? Care must be taken with the statistics, because of the large number of independent variables. (Problems of multicollinearity, plus a sharp reduction in sample size, appear likely.) It might be prudent to keep one foot on the ground and begin with the simple correlation matrix.

In table 5.1 is reported the bivariate correlation (r) of the dependent variable, vote intention, with each of the noneconomic issue variables, plus the three central economic variables for comparison. (The issue items were not posed in the Spanish survey.) At a glance, one sees that certain issues appear especially salient in certain countries. For example, in France, the issue of "employee rights" correlates .34 with vote intention. In Britain, the topic of

TABLE 5.1   Bivariate Correlations (*r*) between Issues and Vote
Intention, 1984

Issues	Britain	France	Germany	Italy
Economic				
Government on economy (X_4)	.60*	.30*	.48*	.23*
Future policies (X_5)	.63*	.44*	.48*	.24*
Anger (X_6)	.51*	.36*	.38*	.20*
Noneconomic				
Community government	−.09*	.05	−.12*	.00
Neighborhood safety	−.12*	−.01	.01	.04
Housing	−.12*	−.02	−.11*	−.11*
Public services	−.05	−.07	−.11*	−.04
Ecologists	−.01	−.10*	.14*	.06
Violence rising	−.00	−.13*	.00	−.08*
Employee rights	−.27*	.34*	−.30*	−.29*
Censorship	.12*	−.05	.24*	.20*
Solar power	.02	.05	−.10*	.03
Unions needed	−.32*	.33*	−.26*	−.24*
Nuclear power	.23*	−.10*	.31*	.07
Unemployment distressing	−.04	.01	−.11*	−.00
Government intervention	−.28*	−.23*	−.00	.03
Homosexuality	−.06	.03	−.21*	−.15*
Military spending	−.32*	.15*	−.33*	−.22*
Energy crisis	−.14*	−.00	−.07*	−.04
Income inequality	−.34*	.28*	−.30*	−.17*
Abortion	−.06	.26*	−.26*	−.34*
Racism	−.04	.05	−.04	−.02
Immigrants	.04	−.20*	.11*	−.05
Peace movement	−.26*	.10*	−.28*	−.18*
Europe unity	−.17*	−.07*	.02	−.13*

*Indicates statistical significance at .05, two-tail.
Note: The vote intention variable carries the usual 0–1 coding. The full wording and codes for each of the issue items appear in the codebook for Euro-Barometer No. 21. The position locations, in order beginning with "community government" are as follows: 31, 32, 33, 36, 52, 136, 137, 141, 143, 145, 147, 148, 149, 150, 151, 152, 153, 155, 157, 160, 161, 196.

"reduced military spending" is associated at .32 with vote. In Germany, the question on the "necessity of nuclear power" produces a correlation of .31. For Italy, "attitudes toward abortion" are associated at .34 with voter preference. It seems, even from such preliminary results, that issues other than economics could influence Western European electorates.

But these correlations represent the strongest in the data set on noneconomic concerns. The other social and cultural issues generally exhibit much less strength. Indeed, about one-half of the correlations do not achieve statistical significance (.05, two-tail). Further, even fewer achieve substantive significance. To illustrate, the number of correlations for each country that exceed .30 is quite small: Britain (3), France (2), Germany (2), Italy (1). Moreover, none of these issue variables seems substantively significant across four (or even three) nations.

Contrast such results to the correlation of economic issues and vote intention. With regard to magnitude, the economic associations are much heftier (see also table 3.4). Here is the average correlation of the three key economic items ("government on the economy," "future policies," "anger") with the dependent variable: Britain equals .58, France equals .37, Germany equals .45, Italy equals .22. *In a simple correlational analysis, then, economic concerns tower over noneconomic concerns in terms of coefficient size. Furthermore, the substantive significance of economic evaluations, unlike that of noneconomic ones, appears to persist across countries.*

What does the examination of these correlations imply? The first implication, of course, is that noneconomic issues can influence individual voters. The second implication, however, is that economic issues are perhaps even more influential. Given the nonexperimental nature of the data, these are only implications. A multivariate model, with appropriate controls, is needed. Unfortunately, having twenty-five or so independent measures on issues poses a multicollinearity threat. In particular, it is difficult to sort out the precise effect of any single issue variable. An approach that gives some satisfaction here is simply to study the overall effect of the noneconomic issue variables on vote intention and on the parameter estimates of the economic variables.

These considerations point to the respecification of the vote intention equation arrived at previously by adding a set of noneconomic issues, where Vote = f(social cleavages, ideology, economic and noneconomic issues). In table 5.2 are estimates for such an equation. (The total number of independent variables is twenty-eight. Because of their large number, the coefficients of the noneconomic issue variables are not listed individually.)

What about the role of noneconomic issues? Despite the multiple controls this model imposes, several social and cultural issues manage statistically significant effects on vote intention. In each country, three or four such issues managed significant coefficients. However, only one of these, the issue of whether "unions are necessary," reached significance in even three of the four countries. The other significant issues, then, were mostly unique to one country (e.g., "racism" in France; "military spending" in Britain; "the peace movement" in Germany; "abortion" in Italy).

Of course, because of the collinearity problem, it is unfair to conclude that the influence of noneconomic issues is unimportant. (Many t-ratios are undoubtedly depressed, for instance.) To avoid faulty inference, it might be better to consider the influence of the noneconomic issues as a whole, rather than singly. Suppose we examine the increase in explained variance now that the noneconomic variables are added to the vote equation. Specifically, this involves comparison of the R^2 before and after (see tables 4.4 and 5.2). When this is done, the following increases in the R^2 are observed: Britain, .08; France, .06; Germany, .10; Italy, .15. These are nontrivial gains in the variance accounted for. We can safely conclude that noneconomic issues have a notable impact on Western European voters.

More important, for our purposes, is whether the impact of these noneconomic issues reduces, perhaps to zero, the impact of the economic issues. What happens to the size of the economic parameter estimates once the vote equation is respecified to include noneconomic issues? At one extreme, the economic issues could be empirically redundant with the noneconomic issues, in which case the economic coefficients would fall to zero. (This might occur, for example, if the issue items are really all measuring the same thing.) At another extreme, the economic issues could be orthogonal to the noneconomic

TABLE 5.2   A Single-Equation Model of Vote Intention, Including Noneconomic with Economic Issues (OLS), 1984

	Britain	France	Germany	Italy
Government on economy (X_4)	.17***	.01	.14***	.12***
Future policies (X_5)	.09***	.07**	.14***	.08**
Anger (X_6)	.08***	.04**	−.02	.04**
Social class (Z_1)	−.11***	.02	−.07*	−.23***
Religiosity (Z_2)	−.01	−.00	.02	.05**
Ideological ID (Z_3)	.06***	−.14***	.09***	.06***
Constant	−.73***	.90***	−.74**	.32
R^2	.64	.59	.58	.54
N	305	302	280	206

*$p < .10$, **$p < .05$, ***$p < .01$, in the expected direction.

Source: Euro-Barometer No. 21.

Note: Since there are twenty-two noneconomic variables (listed in table 5.1), the individual coefficients are not reported.

Codes: The economic variables "government on economy," "future policies," and "anger" follow the codes in table 4.4, as do the variables on class, religion, and ideology.

issues, in which case the economic coefficients would remain essentially unchanged from the original equation. (This might occur if voters consider social issues completely apart from economic ones.) To see the impact of these controls on noneconomic issues, one can compare the economic slope estimates before (in table 4.4) to the economic slope estimates after (in table 5.2).

What does this comparison show? First, the pattern of statistical significance is basically the same, underlining the consistency and pervasiveness of these economic effects. (The t-ratios are reduced somewhat, of course, compatible with the reduction in sample size.) Second, the economic coefficients maintain essentially the same magnitude. Look at the British case. For the "government on the economy" variable, it goes to .17 (from .14 without noneconomic issues controls); for the "future policies" variable, it goes to .09 (from .13); for the "anger" variables, it stays at .08. Overall, the economic effects remain constant (if not a little improved), regardless of country.

Thus, the hypothesis of spuriousness fails to be sustained. A more fully specified model that includes noneconomic issues does do a somewhat better job of accounting for vote choice. However, in such a model, economic and noneconomic issues turn out to be basically orthogonal. Therefore, the exclusion of the noneconomic issues does not noticeably bias the economic coefficients. *The conclusion is heartening: the strong vote impact from the economic variables (reported earlier) is not an exaggeration produced by exclusion of noneconomic variables.*

Pocketbooks, Social Class, and Interaction Effects

According to the evidence presented so far, Western European electorates do not appear to engage in pocketbook voting. Perhaps, though, this finding is artifactual, springing from the additive formulation of the relationships in the original voting equation. Following classical regression assumptions, the slope of the personal economic variable assesses its effect on vote, independent of the influences of other explanatory variables. But suppose that the effect of this pocketbook variable depends on one of these other explanatory variables? For instance, as first suggested by Weatherford (1978), maybe the effect of economic dissatisfaction depends on social class.

According to Weatherford, the working class is hurt more by national economic downturn, and therefore its members are more likely to vote against the incumbent party. To test this hypothesis, he examines data from the United States, namely, the SRC elections panel from 1956 to 1960, which covers a period of economic recession during the second Eisenhower administration. He shows, first, that working-class individuals had a higher probability of perceiving themselves as "worse off" financially when compared to the middle class. He goes on to demonstrate that these working-class individuals have some consciousness of their economic predicament as a class. The key question is, does this perception, individual and collective, of greater economic grievance on the part of workers translate into pocketbook voting? He divides the data into working-class and middle-class subsamples and regresses vote choice on personal economic condition, plus a party identification control variable. When the two are compared, the finding is that the regression coefficient for the personal economic conditions variable in the working-class subsample is almost twice as large (Weatherford 1978, 930).

What about the Western European situation? Look at a concrete example. A Milan factory worker and a Rome business executive both perceive that their financial situation has "worsened" over the last year. Should not that affect vote intention? According to the results reported to this point, a significant shift in their vote probabilities could not be expected. But is that conclusion persuasive? Maybe so for the business executive, who is still relatively well off and sees little alternative but continued support of a ruling coalition dominated by the Christian Democrats. However, the factory worker lives in more economically hard-pressed circumstances and might feel particularly aggrieved to be experiencing financial decline under a bourgeois government. His vote probability could easily shift away toward the Communist opposition. Generalizing the example, the expectation might be that voter response to economic adversity varies with their class standing.

TABLE 5.3   Testing for Interaction Effects between Social Class and Personal Finances (OLS), 1984

	Britain	France	Germany	Italy
National economy (X_2)	.04***	.02	.03	.04**
Government on self (X_3)	.05**	.02	.04	.00
Government on economy (X_4)	.14***	.00	.11***	.07**
Future policies (X_5)	.13***	.07**	.12***	.03
Anger (X_6)	.08***	.04**	.04*	.02
Social class (Z_1)	−.02	.12*	.08	−.30***
Religiosity (Z_2)	.00	−.00	.03**	.09***
Ideological ID (Z_3)	.06***	−.14***	.10***	.08***
Personal finances × class ($X_1 \cdot Z_1$)	−.02	−.03	−.03	.05
Constant	−.83***	.92***	−.92***	−.30***
R^2	.56	.54	.49	.40
N	453	401	433	328

$*p < .10, **p < .05, ***p < .01$, in the expected direction.

Source: Euro-Barometer No. 21.

Codes: The variables from the original model are coded as in table 4.4. The interaction term (personal finances × class) uses the class variable from table 4.4 and the original personal finances variable in table 4.1.

Given this hypothesis—social class heightens or dampens pocketbook effects—an interactive model, with the personal finances variable entering multiplicatively, is called for. In table 5.3 are estimates for the original additive vote equation (see table 4.4), but with a multiplicative term (personal finances × social class) included (Spain is omitted because of measurement differences on the class variable). One observes an absence of statistically significant interactions across the four countries. (The statistical situation worsened still further when the social class variable was "effects" coded [−1,+1] instead of the more customary [0,1] coding.)

Contrary to expectations, the impact of personal finances does not appear to depend upon social class. Workers in financial trouble are no more (and no less) likely to turn that circumstance against the incumbent than are the bourgeoisie. The pocketbook voting hypothesis cannot be saved by considering interactions. More generally, in an effort to find systematic, significant pocketbook interactions, a host of variables—age, ideology, efficacy, religion, gender—were multiplied by personal finances and entered selectively into the original vote equation. Again, no significant interactions were uncovered. The result is unambiguous: *The Western European voter's personal financial situation, either alone or in combination with salient sociopolitical variables, fails to manifest an impact on vote intention.*

The Asymmetry of Economic Effects

The assumption here, as in virtually all the economic voting literature, is that the relationship of economic conditions to vote choice is monotonic; i.e., as economic conditions move from "bad" to "good," support for the incumbent increases. One well-known exception comes from Bloom and Price (1975, 1244), who argue that in the United States "economic conditions have a strong asymmetric impact on the congressional vote. Political parties are 'punished' by the voters for economic downturns but are not 'rewarded' accordingly for prosperity" (also see Claggett 1986). The psychological underpinnings of their argument come from individual research on negative and positive attitudes (Jordan 1965). Unfortunately, Bloom and Price use only aggregate-level elections data (from 1896 to 1970) to defend their thesis. When, more properly, individual-level CPS-SRC surveys are analyzed, no support is found for the asymmetry hypothesis in the American case (Kiewiet 1983, 49).

What about the Western European case? Do voters "punish" the incumbent for a worsening economy, but fail to "reward" it for an improving economy? One straightforward and compelling test of this asymmetry hypothesis highlights the two leading (in a statistical and a theoretical sense) economic variables in the vote equation—"government on the economy" and "future policies." The former is the central retrospective indicator, while the latter is the central prospective indicator. Both ask the respondent to evaluate the effect of government actions as good, bad, or indifferent. In order to test the asymmetry hypothesis, these variables can be "dummied" (with the "indifferent" category as the baseline), and entered into a regression equation, thusly:

$$\text{Vote} = a_1 + b_1R_1 + b_2R_2 + c_1F_1 + c_2F_2 + e \qquad (5.1)$$

where Vote = incumbent-opposition vote intention, as before; R_1 = government effect on economy last year (1 = "good," 0 = otherwise); R_2 = government effect on economy last year (1 = "bad," 0 = otherwise); F_1 = government effect on economy next year (1 = "improved," 0 = otherwise); F_2 = government effect on economy next year (1 = "worse," 0 = otherwise).

If the Bloom and Price asymmetry hypothesis holds, then the dummy variables for bad effects will have strongly negative coefficients (b_2, $c_2 < 0$), while the dummy variables for good effects will have near-zero coefficients (b_1, $c_1 = 0$). In table 5.4 are the estimates. They do not support Bloom and Price. It is true that when economic matters appear "worse" (prospectively or retrospectively), a significant drop in the probability of an incumbent vote occurs, regardless of country. But the same thing happens (in the opposite direction) when economic matters appear "better." That is, when voters perceive that the government has brought prosperity, or is about to do so, they "reward" it with votes. (It is worth noting that this finding persists in the face of full model specification.)

Hence, the expected pattern of asymmetry fails to emerge in these Western European surveys, as was also the case with the American election surveys.

TABLE 5.4   Testing the Bloom and Price (1975) Asymmetry
Hypothesis (OLS), 1984

	Britain	France	Germany	Italy	Spain
Future (worse)	−.14***	−.30***	−.06*	−.12***	−.18***
Future (better)	.40***	.26***	.38***	.09**	.18***
Past (worse)	−.19***	−.14***	−.07**	−.03	−.05
Past (better)	.26***	.09*	.29***	.19***	.19***
Constant	.32***	.55***	.30***	.68***	.48***
R^2	.50	.22	.35	.08	.17
N	748	686	773	543	518

*$p < .10$, **$p < .05$, ***$p < .01$, in the expected direction.

Source: Euro-Barometer No. 21.

Codes: The variables are dummies (0–1), built from the categories of the original variables "government on economy" X_4, and "future policies" X_5 (see table 4.2).

These electorates are "even-handed" in their economic judgments, voting *for* governments that are liked, *against* governments that are disliked. There is no evidence whatsoever that their vote choices are motivated more by "bad times" than by "good times," as Bloom and Price would have us believe. Indeed, the coefficients themselves hint that if any asymmetry exists, it is in the direction of "good times." However, it is not necessary to exhaust that intriguing angle in order to affirm an important conclusion: *Western European voters "reward" governments for "good" economic actions (past or anticipated) to at least as great an extent as they "punish" them for "bad" economic actions.*

Summary and Conclusions

In this chapter, various challenges to the accepted specification of the vote equation were posed. Estimation consequences stemming from the possible endogeneity of the ideology were considered. Many noneconomic issues were related to vote intention and incorporated directly into the model. The question of interaction effects was raised, in particular with regard to the impact of social class on pocketbook voting. The Bloom and Price hypothesis of asymmetric economic voting was tested. These explorations were informative and yielded some positive results; e.g., noneconomic issues do matter for Western European voters. However, the previous conclusions on economic voting remain unaltered. Indeed, the robustness of the original model parameter estimates, against these various tests, strengthens the conviction that economic issues matter a great deal to Western European electorates. Exactly how much is the subject to be taken up now.

NOTE

1. Of course, other kinds of economic concerns, which have not been measured here, may also operate on the vote decision. For instance, Conover (1985) raises the possibility that group economic interests may alter preferences. If so, the inclusion of such a variable would probably raise further the overall impact of economic issues. Another point worth making is that the economic evaluations under consideration here essentially reflect short-term shifts at the margins of performance. Obviously, though, major economic shocks or crises also bear on incumbent support. Assessment of such effects poses interesting problems of research design. (For a provocative attack on such problems, see Finkel, Muller, and Seligson 1987.) Long-term economic change may also influence whole political systems, well beyond the electoral arena. For instance, Inglehart (1987) finds that national economic development (as measured by GNP per capita) relates highly to changing political culture (one measure of which is "mass life satisfaction").

Chapter 6

Economic Forces and European Electorates:
The Contemporary Impact

> In October 1982 the ruling coalition of Christian Democrats, Christian Socialists and Liberals took power with promises of a growth-oriented economy. (Ludolf von Wartenberg, *Wall Street Journal*, July 11, 1984, 25)

> Unless it [the economy] grows much faster, the coalition government of Mr Helmut Kohl will probably lose the federal elections in early 1987. (*Economist*, May 18, 1985, 11)

We have established that economics influences Western European electorates. Exactly how strong is that influence? Do economic evaluations move voters a lot or a little? Which evaluations are more determining? How much does economics shift voter probabilities as compared to the other major forces of social cleavage and partisan ideology? What is the overall effect on governments, as opposed to individuals? Can changes in economic policy perceptions easily topple the ruling coalition? For office holders wishing to maintain power, what economic target is more important—inflation or unemployment?

These questions are pursued below. After the economic effects are assessed by themselves, they are compared to cleavage and ideology effects. Then, estimates are made concerning the impact of shifting individual attitudes on national vote totals. Finally, to complete the discussion of effects, direct and indirect, a multiequation model of vote choice is offered. In that context, the issue of an inflation versus an unemployment policy target is developed.

Economic Effects on Individual Vote Choice

How important are the economic variables as determinants of parliamentary vote intention? A preliminary answer comes from inspection of the standardized regression coefficients of the original model in table 6.1. Looking at the significant coefficients for the three critical economic variables, the median beta weight rests at a respectable value, about .15. Further, because of the

Model 6.1 looks at how important economic variables are as determinants of parliamentary vote intention

standardization, comparison of effects is facilitated. The average beta weights for each of these variables, across all nations, is as follows: "future policies" equals .16, "anger" equals .13, "government on economy" equals .09. While the impact of each is not dissimilar, these values suggest that the prospective evaluation perhaps exercises a slightly greater impact.

These comparisons are useful, providing a common (standard deviation) unit to gauge change. Unfortunately, they may be unreliable, because of differing variances in the independent variables across countries. For that reason, the unstandardized regression coefficients offer more surety. Also, they allow rather precise estimates of effects once the equation is treated as a linear probability model. (Of course, this gain in interpretation may have efficiency costs; Berry and Lewis-Beck 1986; Aldrich and Nelson 1986.) In particular, let us explore the apparently potent effects of the prospective economic evaluation variable. The question is, "What happens to the probability of an incumbent vote, given the elector's evaluation of future economic policy changes from "worse" to "improved"? According to the slope coefficients in table 4.4, the impact in Britain is greatest, with the probability of an incumbent party vote increasing by 26 percent. (That is, the relevant coefficient for the British equation in table 4.4 is .13, indicating that a shift of two units—crossing the middle category and going from "worse" to "improved"—changes the probability by .26.) The impact of such a manipulation is also clear elsewhere: Germany, 24 percent; Spain, 22 percent; France, 12 percent; Italy, 6 percent. Thus, future expectations about what economic performance the government will deliver emerge as a decisive individual vote determinant in Western European electorates.

Furthermore, these future expectations appear to edge out the direct impact of traditional retrospective evaluations. Since both variables have three

TABLE 6.1   Full Single-Equation Voting Model (OLS standardized coefficients), by Nation, 1983 and 1984

	Britain	France	Germany	Italy	Spain
National economy (X_2)	.01	.07*	−.01	.03	.09**
Government on self (X_3)	.07**	.04	−.01	−.02	.04
Government on economy (X_4)	.18***	.04	.13***	.05	.07*
Future policies (X_5)	.31***	.07*	.14***	.10**	.17***
Anger (X_6)	.19***	.08**	.18***	.06*	.15***
Social class (Z_1)	−.05*	.09***	−.11***	−.16***	.11**
Religiosity (Z_2)	.02	.04	−.05	−.14***	.01
Ideological ID (Z_3)	.16***	−.54***	.39***	.53***	−.26**

$*p < .10, **p < .05, ***p < .01$, in the expected direction.

Sources: For Britain, France, Germany, and Italy, the data are from Euro-Barometer No. 20 (on codes, see table 4.2). For Spain, the data are from Euro-Barometer No. 21 (on codes, see table 4.4).

categories, a comparison of their unstandardized slopes is feasible. The retrospective variable certainly is able to alter vote probabilities. Its average unstandardized slope across these nations is .07, indicating that an evaluation shift of government economic policy from "bad" to "good" heightens the incumbent vote probability by 14 percent (see the "government on economy" coefficients in table 4.4). Still, the impact of prospective evaluations is greater. More particularly, the estimated linear probability shifts from changing prospective evaluations exceed those from the retrospective evaluations. (The only exception here is for Britain in table 4.4, where they look about equal in effect.) The following generalization seems warranted: *For legislative elections in these Western European countries, prospective economic policy evaluations have at least as strong an immediate effect on individual vote choice as retrospective economic evaluations do.*

prospective
evaluation
cause
a greater
impact

The Relative Importance of Economic Effects

It is time to take stock, and compare the effects of economics to those from the other central electoral forces—social cleavages and ideological identification. Do changes in economic evaluations move individual voters more than changes, say, in ideology? According to the standardized coefficients in table 6.1, this Left-Right self-placement generally exercises a greater influence than any of the other variables (average beta weight = .38). The finding is not unexpected, given that voters in established industrial democracies tend to follow their long-run "standing decision" for party or ideology. Still, the magnitude of these beta weights might be inflated, owing to the endogeneity problem discussed in chapter 5. Further, concern remains over the meaning of these standardized coefficients across nations. A last difficulty for the purpose of comparison is the varying number of specific indicators for the global concepts under study (i.e., five economic indicators, two cleavage indicators, and one ideology indicator).

so the other forces affecting vote

ideology is strong

   Another strategy for weighing the effect of each set of variables would be helpful. One approach is to exploit the unstandardized OLS coefficients, again utilizing the equation as a linear probability model. In what follows, the probability of incumbent support is calculated for chosen values on the independent variables, and a comparison is carried out between probability changes produced by shifts in ideological position versus social cleavages versus economic forces (see table 6.2). (One problem with such linear probability models is that predictions might fall outside the 0-1 boundaries. A prediction may sometimes be a little exaggerated, e.g., those at the extremes of the curve. Still, this does not seriously compromise our goal of developing *comparative* judgments on effects.)

   With each nation, a baseline prediction for a theoretical voter can be offered and the deviation from it brought about by independent variable shifts compared. As an example, look at the vote probability of Herr Hans Braun, a middle-class German with conservative religious and political views, who believes that the economy is "so-so." (More exactly, he holds the following scores on the independent variables in table 4.2: occupation = 0; religion = 1; ideology = 9; each government effect variable = 2; national economic situation and anger over government = 3.) The likelihood of Hans, or someone with the same scores, declaring a vote for the incumbent Christian-Democrat-led coalition is .86. Suppose, though, that for some reason Hans is obliged to get a blue-collar occupation, becomes less conservative in politics and religion, and develops a generalized sense of economic discontent. (That is to say, his marks on the independent variables change as follows: occupation = 1; religion = 2; ideology = 6; each economic variable = 1.)

What is the impact of these shifts? The change in ideology to the middle of the scale lowers the likelihood of an incumbent vote by 30 percent. The loss of religious conservatism and white-collar employment, together, decrease the probability of an incumbent vote by 15 percent. The combined discontents over the economy drops incumbent loyalty by 36 percent, just slightly more than the ideological change. From these calculations, then, it appears that shifts in ideology and economics exert similar influences on the German voter, followed by the influences of the social cleavage variables.

Such a scenario of vote probability change can be developed for the other nations (table 6.2). Some general findings emerge. *Changing economic conditions exert a force on Western European voters that approaches and sometimes*

TABLE 6.2   Estimated Vote Probability Shifts from a Change in Values in Different Sets of Independent Variables in the Full Single-Equation Model, by Nation, in Percentage

| | Vote Probability Shift | | | | |
	Britain	France	Germany	Italy	Spain
Change in ideology[a]	12	36	30	36	18
Change in social position[b]	3	13	15	28	16
Change in economics[c]	54	25	36	16	39

Sources: The estimates for Britain, France, Germany, and Italy are calculated from table 4.2, and those for Spain are calculated from table 4.4.

[a]Change in the ideological Left-Right self-placement score from 9 to 6.

[b]For the first four countries, change in the social class score from middle class (0) to working class (1), and in the religiosity score from religious person (1) to not a religious person (2); for Spain, because of coding differences, comparable changes are from (2) to (4) on social class and from (1) to (6) on religiosity.

[c]Change in the scores on all the economic variables from a neutral position to a position of discontent (1).

sometimes economic conditions exceeds other issues including ideology [handwritten annotation]

exceeds the force of more traditional factors. More particularly, the vote probability impact of economic evaluations rivals that of ideological identification (with the clear exception of Britain, where economics dominates). Further, economic conditions appear to exercise a greater influence on vote choice than social class and religion (except in Italy).

National Electoral Effects of Individual Economic Change

From the foregoing analysis, the individual Western European voter appears substantially affected by shifting economic circumstances. But do these important individual-level influences add up to something important for the system as a whole? In a given election, could the economic impact on individual voter preferences be expected to sum to a nontrivial shift in the national election outcome? After all, strong individual effects are compatible, under certain circumstances, with only mild effects on national election outcomes (Markus 1988). Let us pose the question in a practical way: what percentage of the total vote should the incumbent expect to lose, if a portion of the electorate becomes economically discontented?

From one election to the next, the public's perception of economic policy and performance varies, on occasion greatly. Sometimes voters think the economy is fine, sometimes not. With these European surveys, it is not possible to track much variation in perceptions over time. However, it is possible to observe cross-sample variation on such items (recall the frequency distributions in table 3.2). Especially interesting is the variation in the "future economic policies" variable (X_5), which was discovered to be surprisingly potent (see table 6.3). The range is considerable, from only 16 percent who saw future economic policies as "improving" (in France) to fully 55 percent (in Spain). Further, the ratio of "worse"/"improved" responses varies from almost 2:1 in France to less than 1:3 in Spain.

These examples are brought forward in order to suggest a reasonable benchmark, in terms of what percentage of the voting public might possibly disaffect to the category of "economic malcontent" from one election to the next. Let us suppose, that economic hard times led a group of voters to switch their prospective evaluations of government economic policy from "improved" to "worse," causing an overall 20 percent increase in the share of the electorate in the "worse" category. If this happened in each of our five countries, what would be the expected incumbent vote loss, ceteris paribus? Here are the estimates of the incumbent vote loss, based on the slope coefficients for X_5 in table 4.4: Britain, -5.2 percent; Germany, -4.8 percent; Spain, -4.4 percent; France, -2.4 percent; Italy, -1.2 percent. (The method of calculation is similar to that for the "level-importance" statistic in Achen

1982, 71–73; e.g., for Germany, expected incumbent vote loss = [20 × (.12 × 2)] = 4.8).

These estimated aggregate shifts in national election returns are consequential, even though resulting from the changed collective economic perceptions of only a modest portion of the electorate. (Of course, the estimated aggregate effects would be still greater if more people were affected, if the other economic evaluations showed similar deterioration, or if the parameter estimate increased.) The impact differs across nations, but always the amount could bring down governments. The estimated shift in the French case, one of the smallest, illustrates this point well. In 1974, Mitterrand received 49.2 percent of the total vote on the second ballot of the presidential race, thereby losing to Giscard. But in 1981, Mitterrand garnered 51.8 percent in the second ballot, thereby defeating Giscard. The shift that moved Mitterrand from the losing column to the winning column was sufficient, although it amounted to no more than 2.6 percentage points. Further, from survey evidence at the time, it has been argued that this shift in election results from 1974 to 1981 was induced by a clear addition of voters to the economically disaffected category. (Specifically, before the Mitterrand election, the European Community Consumer Survey subjective index of national economic well-being measured a record low of just 77 for France; Lewis-Beck 1983, 357.) In this real-world example, then, individual-level effects translated into moderate aggregate

TABLE 6.3   Frequency Distribution on the Effect of Future Government Policies (X₅) on the Economy, by Nation

	Britain	France	Germany	Italy	Spain
A. Euro-Barometer No. 20, 1983					
Improved	30%	24%	20%	28%	55%
No effect	43	54	59	44	31
Made worse	27	23	20	28	14
Total	100%	100%	100%	100%	100%
N	928	924	984	941	754
B. Euro-Barometer No. 21, 1984					
Improved	30%	16%	23%	32%	48%
No effect	44	56	62	46	29
Made worse	26	27	14	22	23
Total	100%	100%	100%	100%	100%
N	965	901	927	915	800

Note: The full item wording and codes appears in table 3.1. The percentages may not sum exactly to 100% due to rounding.

effects which, given the balance of French electorate forces, produced a major change in government. Thus, even at the extreme of the French case, individual economic perceptions may aggregate into a nontrivial, even decisive, influence on the electoral fate of ruling coalitions.

A Multiequation Model of the Western European Vote: The Importance of Indirect Influences

With respect to the American example, multiequation models of the vote have become numerous (classic examples are Fiorina 1981, chap. 9; Jackson 1975; Markus and Converse 1979; Page and Jones 1979). For the study of Western European elections, however, similar models are almost nonexistent, in part because of the shortcomings of the survey data available. In fact, efforts that try to build political economic theory into a general system of equations on Western European vote choice are simply absent. Obviously, a gain from a multiequation effort would be better specification of the vote calculus. In particular, the indirect effects of the variables could be traced, besides the direct effects charted above. We could find out not just what immediately impacts on vote but, more roundabout, what impacts the factors that immediately impact the vote. Hence, a more precise assessment of the comparative importance of the explanatory variables becomes feasible. For example, the single-equation model (as in table 4.4) denies the chance for the economic variables to shape each other and by such means finally to exert yet more influence on the vote decision. However, upon reflection, it seems clear that certain of these economic factors must be dependent on others. The two principal suspects are the global prospective (X_5) and retrospective (X_4) assessments of government economic performance. Let us look at each in sequence.

The prospective question, "Do you think that, a year from now, the government's policies will have improved the country's general economic situation?" unambiguously instructs the respondent to reflect on the future. Most European voters, it would seem reasonable to suppose, base future expectations partly on observance of the past. In particular, in considering how well the government will handle the economy a year from now, they inspect how well it has performed during the last year. Such a process is certainly suggested in some survey evidence on United States elections from 1974 and 1976 (Fiorina 1981, 145–148). More specifically, how might the ties between past and future evaluations be forged? I would hypothesize links much like those in the vote function of equation 4.1. The stylized voter, M. Jean Q. Citizen, regards the past economic circumstances of himself and his nation and responds, cognitively and emotionally, to the impact of government. These retrospective judgments, coupled with his long-run attachments to class, religion, and ideology, contribute to his prospective judgment of government economic performance. With reference to the Euro-Barometer data, this equation is suggested:

$$\text{future policies} = c_0 +$$
$$c_1 \text{ personal finances} +$$
$$c_2 \text{ national economy} +$$
$$c_3 \text{ government on self} +$$
$$c_4 \text{ government on economy} +$$
$$c_5 \text{ anger} +$$
$$c_6 \text{ social class} +$$
$$c_7 \text{ religiosity} +$$
$$c_8 \text{ ideological identification} \qquad \textbf{(6.1)}$$

where "future policies" = X_5, "personal finances" = X_1, "national economy" = X_2, "government on self" = X_3, "government on economy" = X_4, "anger" = X_6, "social class" = Z_1, "religiosity" = Z_2, "ideological identification" = Z_3, and all the variables are measured as in tables 4.1 and 4.4.

Table 6.4 shows estimates for this equation. On the basis of these findings, future expectations concerning government economic performance appear influenced by judgments on past performance. The prospective economic variable (X_5) is significantly determined by all the retrospective (X_2–X_4, X_6)

TABLE 6.4   Future Economic Policies as Dependent Variable (X_5) (OLS), by Nation, 1984

	Britain	France	Germany	Italy	Spain
Personal finances (X_1)	−.01	0.05*	−.06	.03	.09**
National economy (X_2)	.06**	0.11***	.13***	.09***	.22***
Government on self (X_3)	.11**	0.18***	.17***	.10**	−.17
Government on economy (X_4)	.36***	0.23***	.28***	.26***	.28***
Anger (X_6)	.11***	0.05**	.16***	.13***	.08***
Social class (Z_1)	−.08**	−0.13	−.09**	.03	.05*
Religiosity (Z_2)	.00	−0.01	.02	.04*	−.01
Ideological ID (Z_3)	.06***	−0.07***	.03***	−.02	.05***
Constant	.43***	1.18***	.34***	.76***	.36**
R^2	.46	.36	.52	.23	.35
N	541	484	477	471	499

$*p < .10, **p < .05, ***p < .01$, in the expected direction.
Source: Euro-Barometer No. 21.
Codes: The dependent variable is "future policies," (X_5). All the codes are the same as in table 4.4.

economic variables (save the personal finances variable, X_1). On studying these slope coefficients, the biggest impact is delivered by the complex retrospective item (X_4), which aims to measure the government's effect on the national economy over the past year (the average X_4 coefficient = .28). To a certain degree, then, voters' views on what government will do economically are derived from their views on what it did. Such a result implies a modest adjustment to the interpretation that rested just on the single-equation model. *Even though the direct effect of the prospective evaluation is larger than that of the retrospective evaluation, the latter exerts an additional, more subtle effect on vote intention via its influence on the prospective evaluation. The net effect of the two types of evaluation on the vote, then, roughly evens out.*

What determines this retrospective variable (X_4) itself? After all, in explaining economic voting, the role of retrospective evaluation is central. Recall that the survey item used here is "complex"; i.e., the respondent must assess an event (economic performance) and its political management (government policies). These complex retrospective judgments would appear to be functions of simpler, less global judgments (cf. Fiorina 1981, chap. 6). That is, this evaluation of past government economic performance (complex retrospective = X_4) should be partially determined by general past economic performance (simple retrospective = X_2) and specific past economic performance (e.g., inflation, X_8, and unemployment, X_9, which are less global).

Including these more specific economic performance variables, along with the other relevant predictors already considered yields the following specification of retrospective government policy evaluation:

$$
\begin{aligned}
\text{government on economy} = \; & a_0 + \\
& a_1 \text{ personal finances} + \\
& a_2 \text{ national economy} + \\
& a_3 \text{ government on self} + \\
& a_4 \text{ anger} + \\
& a_5 \text{ government on job} + \\
& a_6 \text{ government on inflation} + \\
& a_7 \text{ government on unemployment} + \\
& a_8 \text{ social class} + \\
& a_9 \text{ religiosity} + \\
& a_{10} \text{ ideological identification} \quad \textbf{(6.2)}
\end{aligned}
$$

where the dependent variable of "government on the economy" = X_4, the variables "government on job," "government on inflation," "government on unemployment" = X_7, X_8, X_9, respectively (for codes see table 3.1); the other variables are defined as in equation 6.1.

In table 6.5 are the estimates for this equation. The results show that retrospective evaluation of government economic policy is significantly influenced by the voter's general evaluation of the national economy (X_2). In addition, the less global evaluations of government effect—on individual job security (X_7), inflation (X_8), unemployment (X_9)—are all significant influences. Finally, besides these cognitive evaluations, the affective side of the ledger (anger = X_6) seems to have an impact. Although none of these variables has an overwhelming impact on its own, *together they suggest that simple, and rather specific, evaluations strongly contribute to a total view of government economic management.*

Considering all the economic variables, there is just one that does not behave as expected, and that is the personal finances item (X_1). Nowhere does the deterioration of personal economic circumstances significantly reduce favorable evaluations of past government policy. Thus, indirect effects are missing, which strengthens the earlier conclusion that personal economic conditions have no effect at all on the vote. (Moreover, the conclusion continues to stand when the other measures of personal finances—see table 4.1— are substituted.) So far, the various tests with the pocketbook items in these European surveys have yielded remarkably consistent, negative results. Among Western European electorates, simple retrospective pocketbook evaluations produce negligible shifts in government support.

TABLE 6.5   Past Economic Policies as Dependent Variable (X_4) (OLS), by Nation, 1984

	Britain	France	Germany	Italy	Spain
Personal finances (X_1)	−.06	.00	−.01	.00	.01
National economy (X_2)	.22***	.16***	.20***	.19***	.24***
Government on self (X_3)	.18***	.12***	.02	.02	.06
Anger (X_6)	.09***	.09***	.10***	.05**	.04**
Government on job (X_7)	.07**	.06*	.15***	.14***	.07
Government on price (X_8)	.07**	.01	.18***	.24***	.13**
Government on unemployment (X_9)	.16***	.24***	.27***	.32***	.33***
Social class (Z_1)	−.06	.04	−.01	.17	.00
Religiosity (Z_2)	.00	.00	.00	−.02	.01
Ideological ID (Z_3)	.06***	−.03***	.02*	.04***	.03***
Constant	.08	.61***	−.02	−.02	−.27
R^2	.51	.38	.48	.36	.38
N	518	470	442	462	520

*$p < .10$, **$p < .05$, ***$p < .01$, in the expected direction.

Source: Euro-Barometer No. 21.

Codes: The additional variables "government on job," (X_7), "government on price," (X_8), and "government on unemployment," (X_9) are scored 3 = good, 2 = not much difference, 1 = bad. The wording of these items is in table 3.1. The dependent variable is "government on economy," (X_4). This and the other variable codes are as in tables 4.1 and 4.4.

When could personal finances play a role?

Of course, this does not mean that personal finances could never play a role. Under a restricted set of conditions, it might exercise some very subtle influence on legislative vote intention. In particular, when the voter's judgment of personal finances is "complex," i.e., when it is attributed to government action, then it may have some indirect effect. Observe that, in the above estimated equations, retrospective and prospective evaluations of government economic management may be significantly determined by evaluations of how government has affected personal circumstances (see the coefficients for X_3 in tables 6.4 and 6.5).

For example, if French voters perceive that government action has damaged their own financial well-being, then they are more likely to conclude that future national economic policy will be poorly executed (the significant coefficient for "government on self," X_3, is .18 in table 6.4). In turn, this depressed evaluation of future economic policy will lower the probability of a proincumbent vote (the significant coefficient for "future policies," X_5, is .06 in table 4.4). *By this indirect path personal economics could express itself at the ballot box. However, its actual importance for individual European voters would be extremely small.* (Suppose the first coefficient is multiplied by the second; the estimated probability shift in vote intention resulting from this compound path is tiny; .18 × .06 = .011.) This, then, is the thin thread of truth in the pocketbook voter hypothesis for Western European publics.

The Unified Model

Three key equations have now been reviewed—for vote intention (V), for future government effect on the national economy (X_5), and for past government effect on the national economy (X_4). Taken together, they form a system of equations that purport to explain vote choice in these five Western European nations. The model can be summarized as follows:

$$(X_4) = f(X_1-X_3, X_6-X_9, Z_1-Z_3) \tag{6.3}$$

$$(X_5) = f(X_1-X_4, X_6, Z_1-Z_3) \tag{6.4}$$

$$(V) = f(X_2-X_6, Z_1-Z_3) \tag{6.5}$$

where the x_4, "government on the economy," equation is defined and estimated in table 6.5; the X_5, "future policies," equation is defined and estimated in table 6.4; the V, "vote intention," equation is defined and estimated in table 4.4.

If the model is recursive, i.e., one-way causation and uncorrelated error terms across equations, then the foregoing OLS estimates (tables 4.4, 6.4, 6.5) are preferred over two- or three-stage least squares procedures. Obviously, a nonrecursive assumption would require fewer constraints. Specifically, ideological identification (Z_3) could be treated as endogenous, and the possible economic impacts on it determined. Lamentably, attempts to relax the recursive assumption and explicitly model ideology as an endogenous variable were unsuccessful. (More particularly, because of the small number of exogenous variables at hand in the Euro-Barometer surveys, it appears impossible to develop an instrumental variable for ideology, a Z_3 "hat," that produces sensible two-stage least squares estimates.) Still, accommodating to the recursive constraint, the model serves as a first pass, going beyond the atheoretical, single-equation models that dominate the economic voting literature.

Figure 6.1 sketches the causal flow of political-economic thinking that the system of equations implies. (To facilitate clarity, the noneconomic variables are not sketched.) In examining the path estimates from the equations themselves (represented in tables 4.4, 6.4, 6.5), it would be observed that, for all the nations, the indirect effects from the noneconomic variables are relatively less important than their direct effects on vote intention. (Consider the weakness of the noneconomic variable coefficients in tables 6.4 and 6.5, compared to their coefficients in table 4.4.) *Hence, the earlier judgments on the importance of economic forces, in comparison to social cleavages and ideology, remain essentially intact.* If anything, a careful calculation of "total effects" would imply that economics is even more important than before (Lewis-Beck and Mohr 1976). But given the possible problems associated with the recursive assumption for the model, it would seem better not to force that conclusion.

Inflation versus Unemployment: Which Is More Important?

In the political economy literature, the relative importance of the different economic variables is continually debated, especially with the aggregate time series models. What has a bigger impact on voters, inflation or unemployment changes? My individual-level survey-based models suggest voters respond more to global evaluations of economic performance than to specific components. That is, they do not decide solely on the basis of inflation, unemployment, trade, interest rates, or the national debt. Instead, they make an overall judgment about government economic performance, then vote accordingly. Certainly, though, specific evaluations may, and in fact do, contribute to the general evaluation.

As table 6.5 indicated, global assessment of past government economic policies (X_4) is shaped by specific judgments on inflation (X_8) and unemployment (X_9). However, the weights vary a good deal (especially when both Euro-Barometers are examined). For the unstandardized regression coefficients of the inflation variable ("government on price"), the range is from .01 to .24;

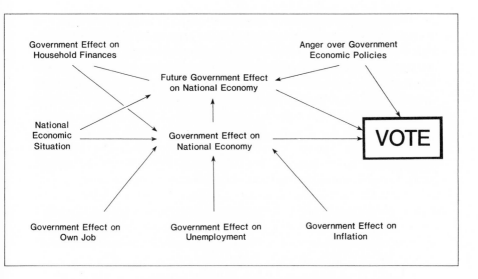

Fig. 6.1.   A diagram of economic voting

and for the unemployment variable ("government on unemployment"), the coefficients range from .11 to .39 (both variables have three-point scales). Further, while the impact of a unit change in employment tends to exceed that of inflation from country to country, exceptions do exist. In Britain, for example, the inflation coefficient (.14) exceeds the unemployment coefficient (.11) with Euro-Barometer No. 20. Moreover, in Italy, the closeness of the inflation-unemployment coefficients hints that their impact may be roughly equal.

These results imply that voters give varying weights to specific economic conditions as they move from one election to the next. In certain election years, perhaps they are most sensitive to inflation when arriving at an overall economic judgment; in other years, it may be unemployment (or trade, etc.). This interpretation seems in line with the inference Chappell and Keech (1985) have made from aggregate data on the U.S. case. Supposing the scenario to be broadly accurate, the task of finally tagging the most important particular macroeconomic indicator is hopeless. Instead, researchers should concentrate on locating global measures of economic policy and performance that capture the shifting weights of their component parts.

Summary and Conclusions

Economics acts as a major force in the movement of contemporary Western European electorates. Changing perceptions of national economic performance can produce substantial shifts in the vote probabilities of individual citizens. Indeed, altered economic evaluations have an impact that approaches, even exceeds, comparable changes in the more traditional anchors of class, religion, and Left-Right ideology. These individual effects manage with little trouble to aggregate into national effects that could bring down governments. Beyond doubt, no issue (or set of issues) facing Europeans today approaches in importance that of the economy.

Could noneconomic variables aggregate together to bring down a government?

are economic variables more impactful than economic variables?

Chapter 7

Across the Nations: Similarities and Differences

Question: Was economics going to be the decisive issue this year? (Ohio homemaker)

Answer: Economics, I cheerfully pointed out, has always been important. (Lindley H. Clark, Jr., economics columnist, *Wall Street Journal*, July 31, 1984, 31)

This investigation differs from virtually all other investigations of economics and elections in that it is not the study of a single country. Rather, a general model of vote choice for Western European electorates is developed and estimated on data from Britain, France, Germany, Italy, and Spain. The approach is "transnational," motivated by the notion that economic voting should operate in essentially the same way, regardless of the Western democracy in which it finds itself (Eulau and Lewis-Beck 1985, 9). Of course, testing is feasible because the concepts—e.g., economic performance, ideology, voting—have a shared meaning; and, importantly, the measures of these concepts are the same across the five nations (conditions which certainly cannot be taken for granted; see Jackman 1985). How successful is the modeling enterprise? In comparative politics research there is always a tension between the goals of generalization and specificity. On one hand, we want to talk about political behavior globally; on the other hand, we must attend to the nuances of particular cultures. How similar are the findings here across nations? How different?

Cross-national Similarities

While these survey-based estimates do exhibit cross-national differences, the consistency of findings is more impressive. Economic effects on vote intention are important in every country.[1] Further, the same three economic variables dominate the models irrespective of country: the retrospective, prospective, and affective components of policy evaluation. This is strong evidence that the process of economic voting is much the same, whether it occurs in Britain,

France, Germany, Italy, or Spain. Despite the sometimes striking differences in electoral institutions, economic grievance arrives at the ballot box by pretty much the same route.

Moreover, when the whole model is evaluated as a general explanation of vote intention, it fares well. Different estimation procedures (OLS or logit) produce similar conclusions. Further, various specification challenges (excluded variables, possible interactions, asymmetric relationships) are successfully met, giving us confidence that the coefficients are reasonably unbiased, and the goodness-of-fit measures are high and steady across the nations. The model, then, manages an ample and fairly even account of vote choice, regardless of country. Let me summarize findings, with regard to cross-cultural similarities: *In Western European electorates (Britain, France, Germany, Italy, Spain), legislative vote choice is largely a function of economic issues, plus class, religion, and ideology.*

Cross-temporal Similarities

The findings on importance of economic voting generalize across space—the five Western European nations. How well do they generalize across time? Put another way, are economic issues important in every election, or does it depend? The status of economic variables in voting models rests to a great degree on whether they can always be counted on powerfully to move the electorate one way or another. Are economic issues, then, "sometime things"? Or are they perennial and commanding? Perhaps economic issues only matter in "bad" years. Relatedly, maybe economic issues have only become important to voters since the 1970s, when the economic troubles really started. If such is the case, then the findings reported here, based on data from 1983 and 1984, could not serve as a firm basis for generalization to other time periods. If these findings are unique, economic issues may well not deserve a lasting place in any Western European voting model.

How to test these arguments? An efficient, up-to-date approach would be a pooled cross-sectional time series (see Stimson 1985 for a lucid explication). One might combine a long series of parliamentary election surveys, estimating carefully specified, measurement controlled models. Unfortunately, such a length of surveys is not available for these Western European electorates. (For example, although the Euro-Barometers reach back to the 1970s, they do not contain an ongoing set of comparable economic items.) Even for the United States, where data are available, analysis of this type has been carried out only for presidential elections (Markus 1988; Rivers 1988). However, Kiewiet (1983, chap. 6) does analyze, separately, twelve United States congressional election surveys from 1958 to 1980. His results provide a solid starting place.

Let us examine Kiewiet's coefficients on the collective economic evaluation variables in terms of their pattern of statistical significance. First, were these economic judgments more likely to be significant determinants of the vote after 1970? No. (In the six elections before 1970, five of these economic coefficients were significant; exactly the same number were significant in the six elections from 1970.) By implication, the economic turbulence of the 1970s in itself does not appear to have made economics salient for American congressional voters. Rather, economic evaluations were as significant for vote choice before 1970 as after. Second, are economic judgments only significant in years of economic downturn? No. (These collective evaluations are significant in very "bad" economic years, e.g., 1958 and 1976, but also in very "good" economic years, 1964 and 1966.) Economic voting, then, seems able to occur in times of boom as well as times of bust.

This inspection of American survey results, stretched over a sufficient time period, suggests that economic voting is an ongoing component of the legislative voting calculus. It does not look like a "Johnny-come-lately" phenomenon. In testing this possibility for the Western European countries under study, only scattered public opinion surveys are at hand. *But they do indicate the critical importance of economic issues in Western European publics, well before the economic roller-coaster of the 1970s.*

In table 7.1, one finds poll data on the British public and the "main government problems," across the period 1951 to 1970. Economic issues— housing, cost of living, full employment, balance of payments, economic affairs, strikes—always absorb a good deal of attention. Indeed, an economic matter is almost always the number one problem cited. (In only one year did an economic concern fail to score either first or second; in 1954, the "H-bomb," followed by "foreign policy," topped the list.) In table 7.2, one finds comparable data on French public opinion for 1957 to 1969, and again economic issues rank high.

These French and British examples imply that economic topics have been featured on the issue agenda of many European voters at least since the 1950s. How to tie this abiding issue concern to the vote? Lamentably, these rich opinion time series cannot be disaggregated to individual voters. But such aggregated observations on economic perceptions do link, at least indirectly, to voters. Kirschgassner's (1985a, 10–11) work provides a nice demonstration from the German case. He argues that the electorate's *perception* of the general economic situation helps determine the vote. Further, this perception is shaped by *objective* economic conditions (in particular, unemployment and inflation rates). Thus, aggregated economic perception is seen as an intervening variable between objective national economic conditions and the vote. Here are his monthly time series equations, first for Christian Democrat support as a func-

**TABLE 7.1   The Importance of Economic Issues
and Public Opinion in Britain, 1951–70**

Year	Main Government Problem (% "Yes")
1951 (July)	Cost of living (38) Foreign policy (24) Next election (6)
1952 (May)	Cost of living (27) Full employment (14) Financial/production (11)
1953 (June)	Foreign policy (36) Cost of living (17) Housing (9)
1954 (April)	H-bomb (24) Foreign policy (18) Cost of living (17)
1955 (January)	Foreign policy (25) Cost of living (18) Social security (9)
1956 (January)	Foreign policy (32) Cost of living (26) Balance of payments (8)
1957 (January)	Suez (38) Cost of living (20) Oil, fuel (11)
1958 (March)	Housing (23) Economic situation, high prices (22) Disarmament (15)
1959 (January)	Unemployment (25) Economic situation, prices (16) Foreign affairs (15)
1960 (January)	Economic affairs (18) Foreign affairs (17) Defense, Nuclear weapons (13)
1961 (January)	Economic affairs (22) International affairs (18) Colonial affairs (16)
1962 (January)	Economic affairs (24) Defense and armaments (20) International affairs (18)
1963 (January)	Economic affairs (52) International affairs (10) Defense (10)
1964 (January)	Economic affairs (24) Housing (13) International affairs (12)

TABLE 7.1—*Continued*

Year	Main Government Problem (% "Yes")
1966 (March)	Economic affairs (48)
	Housing (16)
	Commonwealth (14)
1968 (February)	Economic affairs (59)
	International affairs (13)
	Labor relations (6)
	Immigrants (6)
1970 (April–May)	Cost of living (35)
	Labor relations (13)
	Other economic affairs (11)

Source: The Gallup International Public Opinion Polls. (Britain). (New York: Random House, 1976).

Note: The figures in parentheses indicate the percentage who identified something in that category as the "main government problem." The problems are ordered by rank.

tion of the perceived general economic situation (GES), and then for GES as a function of the unemployment rate (UR) and the inflation rate (IR).

$$CD_{(t)} = 11.27 + .59CD_{(t-1)} + .20CD_{(t-3)}$$
$$(3.19) \quad (7.92) \qquad (2.79)$$

$$- .07GES_{(t)} + .04GES_{(t-4)} + u_{(t)} \tag{7.1}$$
$$(-4.93) \qquad (2.63)$$
$$\text{Adj.}R^2 = .74 \qquad SEE = 1.40 \qquad 118 \; df$$

$$GES_{(t)} = 13.249 + 1.07GES_{(t-1)} - .22GES_{(t-2)}$$
$$(3.42) \quad (12.28) \qquad (-2.62)$$

$$- 5.38UR_{(t)} + 4.8UR_{(t-4)} - .74Ir_{(t-1)} + u_{(t)}$$
$$(-3.25) \qquad (2.85) \qquad (-1.93) \tag{7.2}$$
$$\text{Adj.}R^2 = .94 \qquad SEE = 3.82 \qquad h = .53 \qquad 117 \; df$$

where CD = monthly opinion poll popularity of the Christian Democrats; GES = aggregated survey perception of the general economic situation; UR = unemployment rate; IR = inflation rate; the figures in parentheses are t-ratios; h = the h-statistic for autocorrelation; the data are monthly observations from February, 1971, to April, 1982; the estimation procedure is OLS.

These results indicate that electoral support varies with national eco-

TABLE 7.2   The Importance of Economic Issues and the French Public, 1957–69

Year	Most Important Problem (% "Yes")
1957 (September)	Algeria (51) Economic situation (26) Domestic situation (20)
1958 (January)	Algeria (37) Financial situation; budget (31) Governmental problems (10)
1959 (February)	Algeria (53) Economic and financial situation (23) Buying power (12)
1960 (March)	Algeria (50) Peace in Algeria (28) Prices (5)
1961 (April)	Algeria (78) Salaries (5) Government stability (4)
1962 (February)	Foreign relations (70) Social welfare (18) Domestic policy (12)
1963 (March)	Social problems; strikes (40) Salaries and prices (27) Foreign policy (11)
1964 (July)	Prices (17) Salaries; standard of living (15) Domestic policy (12)
1965 (May)	Wages (19) Unemployment (16) Housing (12)
1966 (February)	Common Market; Europe (18) Salaries; standard of living (14) Peace in the world (13)
1967 (May)	Unemployment (15) Peace (14) Social problems; education (14)
1968 (May)	Students; demonstrations (21) Unemployment (21) Economic and agricultural (10)
1969 (June)	Salaries; standard of living (21) Devaluation of the franc (14) Government stability (13)

Source: The Gallup International Public Opinion Polls. (France). (New York: Random House, 1976).

Note: The figures in parentheses are the percentages indicating that something in that category is the "most important problem." These problems are ordered by rank.

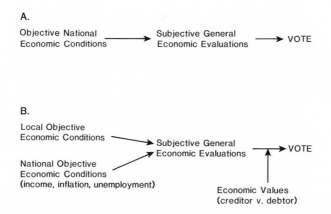

A.

Objective National ——————→ Subjective General ——————→ VOTE
Economic Conditions   Economic Evaluations

B.

Local Objective
Economic Conditions ——————→ Subjective General ——————→ VOTE
                                      Economic Evaluations

National Objective
Economic Conditions
(income, inflation, unemployment)   Economic Values
                                             (creditor v. debtor)

Fig. 7.1. Sketches relating objective and subjective economic conditions to the vote

nomic perceptions, which in turn vary with standard macroeconomic indicators. Once this is granted, macroeconomic indicators may serve as proxies for the (aggregated) collective economic evaluations of voters. If one goes on to argue that aggregated perceptions of the economy are totally determined by the objective conditions, then a simple causal chain model of the vote is suggested, as in figure 7.1A. In such a model, the electoral effects of general economic perceptions are totally determined, in the end, by fluctuations in national economic conditions.

How serviceable is such a model? Can we use, say, national income growth in a time series voting model as a stand-in for perceived economic evaluations? Basically, whether one answers yes depends on how one views the error. At one end, Kramer (1983) implies that a lack of perfect fit between subjective and objective economic measures is due to measurement error or response rationalization (because of partisanship). In other words, the voters "real" economic evaluation (i.e., his or her evaluation net of survey error or partisan bias) is made up entirely of objective fluctuations in national income. If this is the case, then a national income variable could yield unbiased, if somewhat inefficient, aggregate estimates of individual evaluations. That is, the slope coefficient for the income variable in a properly specified aggregate single-equation model of election outcomes would correctly estimate the total effect of economic evaluations on elections. The equation, then becomes essentially a "reduced form" model (with a causal structure compatible to fig. 7.1A).

However, as Kiewiet and Rivers (1984) point out, this error is likely composed of more than noise and rationalization. There are real evaluation differences, due to real differences in experience, that affect perceptions. For example, citizens in different parts of a country may experience different mixes of employment, inflation, and income policies, which lead them to different evaluations of collective economic performance. As Gene Meeker of the Waterloo (Iowa) Chamber of Commerce observed, "For the country, 1983 was a boom year. But for Waterloo, it was the worst" (*Wall Street Journal*, March 28, 1984, 1). Further, even if they experience the same policies, they may assign them different values; e.g., a debtor may care little about inflation, while a creditor cares a lot. Such varied weighting will lead to different judgments in the face of ostensibly the same national economic conditions. These varied perceptions will affect incumbent vote support in ways that aggregate objective economic indicators cannot completely capture. (The actual causal structure is perhaps something like that in figure 7.1B.) Aggregate time series models that exclusively include objective indicators risk underestimating the total effect of economic evaluations on electoral outcomes.

Thus, macroeconomic indicators are imperfect proxies for economic perceptions. Still, they clearly have value, in the absence of better data. Let me try them out on simple hypotheses about the changing importance of economic voting *over time*. Suppose the following naive model of economic voting, which is amenable to estimation with the limited aggregate time series available:

$$\text{Vote} = b_0 + b_1 \text{Economy} + e \tag{7.3}$$

where Vote = the percentage popular vote going to the incumbent (coalition) in the legislative election; Economy = relevant macroeconomic indicator (e.g., unemployment rate, inflation rate, growth rate); e = error.

The live hypotheses revolve around the residuals $(V - \hat{V})$ from this equation, and their relationship to time. What are the germane possibilities? The residuals may be unrelated to time (the null hypothesis, H_0). Or they may be related to time; in particular, the pre-1970 residuals might be greater than the post-1970 residuals (the alternative hypothesis, H_1). The hypotheses can be put somewhat more formally in terms of differences in mean (M) values, because of the limited number of cases (7–8) that empirical testing entails:

$$H_0: M_1 = M_2$$
$$H_1: M_1 > M_2 \tag{7.4}$$

where M_1 = the mean residual score $(V - \hat{V})$ of the above equation, for the observations before 1970; M_2 = the mean residual score $(V - \hat{V})$ of the above OLS equation, for the observations after 1970.

On one hand, if the null hypothesis is rejected, the implication is that economic voting is more important for the post-1970 period. That is, it can account for vote choice better in the later period (hence the lower residuals). The argument that economic voting is transitory, a product of the upheavals of the 1970s, gains weight. Perhaps economics did not really drive electorates until then. On the other hand, if the null hypothesis is not rejected, then the implication is that economic voting was as strong in the pre-1970 period as it is now. That is, it can account for vote choice equally well in either period (as indicated by equivalent mean residuals). In this case, the argument for giving economic variables a permanent place in a general voting model is strengthened.[2]

In table 7.3, the results of these difference of means tests are reported for the Western European nations under study (except Spain), covering the period 1956 to 1984. First, the foregoing simple equation (eq. 7.3) was estimated (OLS) fo. each, with popular incumbent vote share regressed on the leading macroeconomic predictor (selected from among the annual unemployment rate, the inflation rate, or the GDP growth rate; see table 1.4). For instance, recall that in France unemployment was correlated .93 with incumbent party coalition legislative vote share, a higher correlation than for GDP or inflation. Second, the residuals from this equation were calculated and averaged for the pre-1970 and post-1970 elections.

What do the estimates show? There is a slight but consistent difference, with the earlier period carrying somewhat larger residuals. Is this simply due to a change in the overall strength of economic voting? No. Rather, it appears to be a product of the events of 1968. The student-worker unrest that dominated the politics of these nations in and around 1968 is well known. These years were unusual, and that special status is revealed in these residuals. For the

TABLE 7.3   Differences in Mean Residuals, Pre-1970 (M_1) and Post-1970 (M_2), Four Nations

Country	M_1	$(M_1{}^a)$	M_2	Is $M_1{}^a$ > M_2?
Britain	1.9	(1.8)	1.4	negligible
France	1.5	(0.8)	1.0	no
Germany	7.95	(3.3)	4.0	no
Italy	2.6	(1.7)	1.3	negligible

Note: Residuals from a simple macroeconomic model of the vote share, 1956–84. The vote share variable is constructed as in table 1.1. The residuals were derived by regressing this vote variable on the best-fitting macroeconomic predictor: the inflation rate in Britain and Italy, the unemployment rate in France, and the GDP growth rate in Germany; Spain offers too few observations for analysis.

[a]The election nearest 1968 has been excluded; i.e., in Britain, 1970; in France, 1968; in Germany, 1969; in Italy, 1968.

election nearest 1968, the residual stands as an outlier. Suppose these outliers are removed from each series, and the difference of means test recalculated (see table 7.3). Then, the difference in favor of the pre-1970 period essentially disappears. For instance, in the French case when the 1968 election is removed, $M1^a = .8$ (based on 1956, 1958, 1962, 1967 elections), and $M2 = 1.0$ (based on 1973, 1978, 1981). *Barring extreme social upheaval, the implication is that economic conditions reliably determine a good share of the electoral outcome in French legislative elections.*

This conclusion seems to apply to the other countries as well. Once the outliers are excluded, the residual differences become tiny and inconsistent. Of course, such analysis can be no more than suggestive, because of issues of sampling, measurement, and ecological inference. However, it is congruent with the notion that economic conditions have an enduring place in the voter calculus of Western electorates.

Cross-national Differences

While economics is a significant electoral force in each of these Western European countries, its impact is greater in some than in others. In reviewing the many tables, an important distinction repeatedly emerges—economic voting is strongest in Britain, followed by Spain and Germany, then France and Italy. (Recall in particular table 6.2, where vote probability changes are estimated.) Why do the same economic evaluations have a differing impact across these countries?

Undoubtedly, political and economic system characteristics are partly responsible and should be identified. Of course, the search is hampered by the small sample size ($N = 5$). Certain obvious political system characteristics seem poor candidates for explanation, since they exhibit almost no cross-national variation. For instance, all are parliamentary (or modified parliamentary, e.g., France) systems with a dominant lower chamber. Similarly, candidates for office, in contrast to the United States, are largely at the mercy of the parties. They are usually selected by the party, with the parties controlling the parliament. Indeed, Europeans may vote for party lists instead of individuals. The limited degree of candidate autonomy, then, makes it difficult for the candidate to influence the issue agenda. Turning to the economic system, again there is a limited variance problem. In particular, each of these nations is a wealthy industrial capitalist economy.

Nevertheless, potentially relevant system differences do exist. I test hypotheses on four variables (of which two are essentially political, two economic): *coalition complexity, state capacity, open economy*, and *economic growth*. The results are in table 7.4. Looking at the first row, one observes the countries, ranked-ordered according to their individual economic voting strength (from Britain = 1 to Italy = 5). In subsequent rows, the scores on the system variables are ranked, according to country (e.g., on economic openness, from Germany = 1 to Spain = 5). The test is straightforward: to the extent that rank on the system variable is compatible with rank on the economic voting variable, the hypothesis of a system effect is supported. At a glance, some hypotheses appear to receive support, some do not. Below, I discuss the null findings, then the positive ones.

State Capacity

One possible reason for the observed differences in economic voting strength may be that some political systems work better than others. For example, on one hand, suppose a German voter (male) is economically dissatisfied and votes for the opposition SPD, because he feels it can move the state apparatus in the policy direction he prefers. On the other hand, suppose an Italian worker (male) who is economically dissatisfied but does not change parties, because he believes the inefficient state apparatus will not respond.

In other words, states may vary in their capacity, and that helps determine the strength of economic voting. There is evidence that states do so vary. Past comparative research by Putnam (1973, 9) suggested that the British government carried a reputation for "effectiveness, stability, and responsiveness," while the Italian government did not. But these are reputational data, and it is uncertain the characterizations still hold. Whether or not Italy is a "weak" state is debatable, at least if "weakness" is equated with "size" of the public sector (Lewis-Beck 1986c).

Of course, formidable measurement issues surround a global concept like

TABLE 7.4   Hypothesis Tests on Economic Voting Strength and
System-Level Variables (entries are ranks)

	Britain	Spain	Germany	France	Italy
Economic voting strength	1	2	3	4	5
Coalition complexity	1	2	3	4	5
State capacity	3	5	4	2	1
Open economy	2	5	1	4	3
Economic growth	1	2	3	4	5

Note: The measures, with values for each country, from Britain, Spain, Germany, France, Italy, respectively, are as follows. Economic voting = strength of individual economic voting, as measured in table 6.2. State capacity = government expenditures as a percent of GDP in 1983: 40.2, 30.9, 31.1, 44.7, 47.0; IMF (1986). Open economy = exports as percent of GDP in 1983: 26.8, 20.4, 31.5, 22.2, 23.5; IMF (1986). Economic growth = average GDP growth rate, 1980–84: 1.9, 1.4, 1.3, 1.1, 0.9; OECD Economic Surveys 1986/87.

"state capacity." Current discussions over "theories of the state" focus on "capacity," "autonomy," "transformation," and their measurement (see Benjamin and Elkin 1985; Krasner 1984; Lewis-Beck and Squire 1988; Skocpol and Finegold 1982). Here, state capacity is indicated by the size of the public sector (total government expenditures as a percent of GDP). This simple indicator has imperfections. Nevertheless, *the clear expectation is that, to the extent the state is capable of exercising its policy will, the public sector would tend to be relatively larger. Measured thus, state capacity has no relationship to economic voting, according to the results of table 7.4. Stronger states, then, do not necessarily breed stronger economic voting.*

Open Economies

In the political economy literature, much has been made recently of the political impact of "economic openness" (Cameron 1978; Lewis-Beck and Rice 1985b; Lindbeck 1976). How might the dependency of a national economy on foreign trade influence economic voting? Perhaps greater interdependency sensitizes voters to the policies of government, which has a more difficult time stabilizing the economy because of fluctuations beyond the border. For example, many local workers may have jobs tied to international markets. They may be suddenly threatened with layoffs because of an unanticipated shift in international demand. Such voting groups might be unusually aware of how their economic circumstances were connected to trade agreements with other nations. If so, the economic voting coefficients might be greater in nations differentially affected by trade. Not so, on the basis of these results. *In nations that have more open economies (measured by export value as a percent of GDP), there is no tendency to stronger economic voting. In Spain, where the economy is the least open, voters appear as likely to vote on the basis of economic issues as in Germany, where the economy is most open.* While international economic currents are undoubtedly part of the voter calculus in both countries, they do not swamp domestic concerns. Indeed, these results suggest that international economic topics operate along side other economic issues (like unemployment and inflation), indirectly influencing the citizens' overall evaluation of government economic performance, which ultimately shapes the vote.

Economic Growth

In cross-national political studies, the effects of economic growth are frequently examined. A perennial hypothesis, for instance, relates economics to democratic performance (a recent examination appears in Brunk, Caldeira, and Lewis-Beck 1987). With regard particularly to the economic voting literature, variables on national economic growth routinely make their appearance in aggregate models (see chap. 2). These works basically examine the variables at the system (e.g., national) level, without regard for contextual interaction effects. However, one exception deserves more exploration here, that of Bloom and Price (1975, 1244). They contend that economic changes affect U.S. congressional elections in times of recession but not in times of prosperity. In the former, the voter's attention is turned to economic trends, but in the latter, the voter relies more on traditional cues such as party affiliation. To test their interaction hypothesis, they divide the elections into those preceded by a rising income and those preceded by a declining income and estimate the voting function inside each. They find that in the "rising income subsample" the percentage change in real per capita income is not significantly related to the congressional vote, whereas in the "declining income subsample" it is highly significantly related. From this, they draw their well-known asymmetry hypothesis, where voters "punish" the incumbent for economic bad times but fail to "reward" for economic good times.

As demonstrated in chapter 5, this intriguing asymmetry is not actually uncovered within any of these Western European national surveys. European voters who are economically content are at least as likely to vote *for* the incumbent, as economically discontented voters are to vote *against* the incumbent. However, maybe the asymmetry angle is worth pursuing in a slightly different way, and the specific research strategy of Bloom and Price provides a clue. That is, economic growth could be treated as a *contextual* variable. The hypothesis is direct: the strength of *individual* economic voting varies with the *national* rate of economic growth.

The data of table 7.4 nicely support this argument. *When the nation has experienced a higher rate of growth (measured as the average GDP percentage change, 1980–84), the strength of economic voting among the citizenry is higher.* On one hand, the strong economic voting in Britain seems partly due to the relatively higher economic growth they have experienced over the period. On the other hand, the weaker economic voting in Italy is partly a function of the slowed economy. What the context of economic growth tends to do, then, is strengthen the bond (e.g., the slope coefficient) between economic evaluations and the vote.

This result does not spell asymmetry in the Bloom and Price sense. In any given country, the voting likelihood (based on a good versus a bad evaluation) is still symmetric. However, that likelihood may be greater from one country to the next, because of the economic growth context. When the economy is doing well, voters are more likely to take their economic evaluations (good or bad) into account at the ballot box. Of course, this makes good sense and is yet another piece of evidence that individual citizens react systematically to collective economic currents.

Coalition Complexity

Powell (1987) investigates how constitutional designs influence ways citizens control government. Among other things, he examines the consequences of electoral characteristics for governmental accountability in sixteen democratic nations. Two conditions, in particular, seem to encourage voters to "throw the rascals out" if they are dissatisfied: "clarity of responsibility" in making policy and "decisiveness of election outcome." As Powell puts it: "Unless *both* of these characteristics are realized significantly it will be difficult for citizens to know who to hold responsible and/or to put their evaluations into effect . . ." (13).

This multiplicative hypothesis on "collective government accountability" is enticing. And using the scores Powell offers on the two conditions, "clarity" and "decisiveness," it is possible to rank the nations under study here in the following order: Germany, France, Britain, Spain, Italy. (For the calculations, the "clarity" score is multiplied by the "decisiveness" score; see Powell 1987, table A1.) As can be observed, this ranking does not line up well with the "strength of economic voting" ranking (see table 7.4). (This conclusion also holds if the conditions are assessed additively.) Only Italy stays unchanged, continuing to be ranked last in strength of economic voting and degree of collective government accountability.

Nevertheless, Powell's notions of "clarity" and "decisiveness" remain promising. Perhaps the difficulty with this specific test stems from complications of measurement (e.g., for each of these countries, he scored two elections: Germany, 1976, 1980; France, 1973, 1978; Britain, 1974, 1979; Spain, 1979, 1982; Italy, 1976, 1979). As I have argued elsewhere, these cross-national differences in economic voting actually appear to be coming from *diffusion of government responsibility* and from what might be called *incumbent alternatives for dissent* (Lewis-Beck 1986b). The former, similar to Powell's idea on responsibility, argues that with more parties in government it becomes difficult to pin the blame for economic difficulties on any one party. Hence, unable to make a unique partisan attribution of responsibility, the voter does not take economics into account.

The second condition, incumbent alternatives for dissent, can be understood by imagining different scenarios of economic voting. First, suppose a two-party system as a point of reference. When the economically disgruntled voter defects from the incumbent party, the only choice available is the opposition party. Now, suppose a three-party system, with a two-party incumbent coalition. The economically dissatisfied voter might switch from one incumbent party to the other, rather than defect to the third-party opposition. Economic dissatisfaction does not lead to a loss of overall incumbent vote support, in contrast to the two-party system example. Finally, suppose still more parties in the system, with at least three in the incumbent coalition. In this case, the possibilities for economic discontent to express itself, *without* an opposition vote, increase even further. These two conditions, diffusion of responsibility and incumbent alternatives for dissent, can be measured with a simple indicator: number of parties in the ruling coalition. Thus, a general hypothesis, one of *coalition complexity*, is suggested: the more political parties in the governing coalition, the less strong the economic voting.

The hypothesis fits these data neatly. The count of parties in the ruling coalitions of these nations (at the time of the surveys) is as follows: Britain, one party; Spain, one party; Germany, one major party and one minor party; France, essentially two major parties; Italy, two major parties and three minor parties. *This country ranking, by party composition of the incumbent, coincides with the country ranking by strength of economic voting. The number of parties in the ruling coalition appears to dampen the economically based anti-incumbent vote.* Paradoxically, then, in more complicated multiparty systems like Italy and France, even when macroeconomic conditions seem relatively bad, economic dissatisfaction may not spend itself in an opposition ballot, thereby lowering the chances of a change in government economic policy.

But as a caution it is worth keeping in mind that it is not a wealth of parties in the political system per se that diminishes economic voting. Instead, it is the number of parties in the ruling coalition itself that counts. Spain is of course the key test here. With its many national and regional parties, it is clearly the most complex (at least in terms of number) multiparty system under study (on Spanish regional voting, see Lancaster and Lewis-Beck 1985). Nevertheless, during this period there was only one party—the Socialists—in national government. Obviously, it offered a clear target to the economically disgruntled.

Accounting for Cross-national Differences

The above examination of selected hypotheses on cross-national differences in economic voting strength can only be suggestive, based as it is on a sample of five nations. Nevertheless, it stands as useful spadework for future studies. In terms of theories, the following elementary sketch presents itself (fig. 7.2). The dependent variable, individual economic voting strength, is influenced by two contextual variables, one economic and one political. To the extent the nation has a good economic growth record, economic voting is strengthened. Also, the more one-party dominant the ruling coalition, the stronger are economic voting ties. Of course, these two variables are not the sole determinants of economic voting strength. Moreover, they are negatively correlated with each other (as the double-headed arrow in the sketch implies). An interesting implication is that nations with lower economic growth are more likely to have complex party coalitions, both conditions making parliament relatively

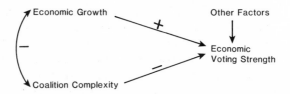

Fig. 7.2. Possible determinants of cross-national differences in economic voting strength

insensitive to economic policy change. Of course, a more fully specified model is needed to delineate the links between economic growth, party coalitions, and the other system-level variables (see the recent exchange between Lange and Garrett [1985] and Jackman [1987]), and that modeling effort should be taken up with estimates on a comparative data-set more elaborate than the one at hand.

Summary and Conclusions

The preceding discussion serves as a reminder of two important things. First, the nations differ in terms of economic voting strength. Second, the bonds between economics and the citizen are mutuable. Shifting coalitions and economic spurts can do much to alter these bonds. With these qualifications in mind, I return to the original question about scientific generalization. What findings on economic voting can be generalized?

The models estimated on the Euro-Barometer surveys (1983 and 1984) indicate that economic issues have an important effect on vote intention in Britain, France, Germany, Italy, and Spain. To what extent is this cross-national finding bound to a particular election or particular period in time? Previously reported estimates from the United States case suggest that the importance of economics persists from congressional election to congressional election. Unfortunately, no direct tests of this question could be carried out for Western Europe. But simple over-time analysis shows that economic matters have been invariably high on the issue agenda of selected Western publics since the 1950s. Further, macroeconomic factors seem equally able roughly to predict election outcomes, regardless of whether the election is pre- or post-1970. (The exception is an election held during a period of extreme social unrest, such as 1968 in France; in such a context, the usual economic forces are overridden.)

In sum, economic issues appear to be prominent and permanent electoral forces in the mass publics of the leading nations of the West. This is really no surprise. As Keynes remarked, "we have been expressly evolved by nature—with all our impulses and deepest instincts—for the purpose of solving the economic problem" (quoted in Levy 1981, not paginated). In other words, economic concerns are always on our agenda, and these days we tend to seek solutions from government. If governments deliver on their economic promises, they are rewarded with votes. If not, they are punished. These facts led Butler and Stokes (1969, 390) to decide that economic issues came "as close as any in modern politics to being pure 'valence' issues." Unlike most other issues, it is one on which there is virtually total consensus. Leaders are elected to bring about prosperity, just as they should "keep the peace" and ensure "good government." If they fail to do so, they can only lose votes. (No one is "for" recession.) Collective economic conditions are nontrivial electoral determinants, across advanced democratic nations and across elections. In models of comparative voting behavior, they deserve careful measurement and inclusion.

NOTES

1. An interesting question, not explored here at all, is the extent to which economic conditions affect elections in semidemocratic systems. Take the example of Mexico, where it has been argued that because of discontent over the 1982 economic difficulties, the conservative PAN opposition made gains against the ruling PRI in subsequent midterm elections. Is there a long-run, observable economics-electoral connection in this one-party dominant system? Indeed, more exaggeratedly, is there an economics-politics link in nondemocratic systems? Perhaps. In his work on East European countries, Lafay (1981b) has discovered that national economic changes are significantly related to changes in the composition of the government leadership.
2. Of course, the pattern of residuals from this aggregate-level analysis cannot speak directly to the change in the magnitude of the individual-level coefficients of the collective economic evaluation variables. Take an example. Suppose a collective economic evaluation variable has a slope coefficient of .3 in a linear probability model estimated from a national election survey. The number of votes this costs the incumbent does indeed depend on this slope magnitude, but it also depends on the portion of the citizenry that shifts to the "worse" category. (This is the group whose probability of voting against the incumbent increases.) Thus, for two elections it is possible to have, at least in theory, two different slopes (say a low one and a high one) yielding the same net vote change (because of differing portions who shift to the "worse" category). (The data analysis in the next section, on cross-national differences, bears on this question of the determinants of individual economic slope differences, from election to election.)

Part 3   The Time Dimension: Retrospective versus Prospective

Chapter 8

Prospective Economic Voting: Further Evidence from American Consumer Surveys

> Are you better off than you were four years ago? (President Ronald Reagan)

> Are we building a better, brighter future? (Senator Paul Simon, presidential challenger, *West Branch Times,* July 16, 1987, 3)

The voter response to economic change, like all human reactions, takes place over time. Does the electorate give primary attention to the economic performance of yesterday, today, or tomorrow? According to Paldam (1981b, 293), there are two perennial questions surrounding the time-preference pattern: (1) "Do people react to past and present economic conditions or to the expected future ones?" and (2) "What is the size of the time-preference parameter, which people use in weighting events in different years?" With regard to the first, these Western European results suggest people react to both. With regard to the second, the prospective and retrospective parameters seem to have about equal weight (at least once indirect effects are taken into account). In this chapter I try to answer these questions for the United States case, where new survey data with multiple-time economic measures have recently become available.

American Evidence on the Timing of Economic Voting

A review of the United States aggregate time series research on the vote function gives many different specifications for the time reaction. Recall that Kramer (1971) specified a lag structure of t-1. That is, the national congressional vote share of the president's party in one year (t) is a function of macroeconomic conditions in the previous year (t-1). Stigler (1973) countered with a congressional voting model that averaged economic conditions from the two previous years, (t-1 + t-2)/2. Tufte (1978, chap. 5), in his House equation, measured per capita income changes in the election year itself (t). All these models have one year as their unit of time. Of course, other units (e.g., quarters, months) are possible. For example, the House forecasting model of

Lewis-Beck and Rice (1984) predicts seat change from, among other things, the quarterly GNP growth rate six months before the election.

The work on popularity functions routinely uses quarterly or monthly data, rather than annual. The length of most popularity series allows rather elaborate specification of the lag structure. One alternative is a geometric pattern, where the coefficients of the economic indicator decline systematically, say, t-1 = .8, t-2 = .4, t-3 = .2, t-4 = .1, suggesting the diminished but persistent influence from the economic activity of earlier periods (e.g., see Hibbs 1982a). Another alternative is a polynomial distributed lag, in which the impact of the economic indicators at first increases as time passes, then decreases; e.g., at t-1 = .2, t-2 = .7, t-3 = .11, t-4 = .8, t-5 = .3. According to Monroe (1978) and Golden and Poterba (1980), this second-order polynomial does indeed accurately describe the relationship in the United States. But Norpoth (1984, 265–68) challenges this specification, arguing it is a simple linear effect from t-1.

A few important things about the time series investigations bear notice. First, they are retrospective models (a refreshing exception is Chappell and Keech 1985). Past economic behavior is viewed as the predictor of current electoral behavior. No direct tests of a prospective decision-making framework are offered. Further, even if the retrospective constraint is accepted, the many studies show no convergence on a particular time frame or form. The likelihood that a consensus will emerge appears small, since the available time series data provide strong quantitative support for many rival models. As has been sagely remarked by Norpoth (1984, 255), "With time series observations being as dependent as they are, correlations between one series of interest (say, popularity) and lagged values of another (say, inflation) can be easily documented . . . ."

Nevertheless, assume that an agreement is reached; e.g., it is national real per capita income from the previous year that makes the statistical difference. Still, we cannot be sure that voters are retrospective and myopic, as that finding implies. From the macrolevel time series, it is simply too risky to infer such microlevel decision-making processes. Of course, recognition of this general limitation of aggregate time series analysis forced the turn to individual level survey research in order to expose economic voting. Interestingly, though, this survey research carried over the retrospective assumption. Partly, this was inspired by the useful body of voting theory laid down by V. O. Key (1966). Also, it seems to have had a very practical origin—the critical economic questions in the Michigan Center for Political Studies–Survey Research Center (CPS-SRC) election studies were phrased retrospectively. Since 1956, the standard personal finances item has followed this phrasing: "During the last few years has your financial situation been getting better, getting worse, or has it stayed same?" With regard to collective items, the following kind of question has been most frequently asked: "Would you say that at present business conditions are better or worse than they were a year ago?"

The impact of these evaluations (and related ones) has already been discussed (see chap. 3). Here, the emphasis is on the time frame of these evaluations. Observe that they permit only a retrospective test, asking the respondent to consider just the last year or two. No assessment of future economic conditions is allowed. Fortunately, this limitation did not go unchallenged, as the efforts of Kuklinski and West (1981) and Fiorina (1981) testify. Let us first consider the former.

In their investigation of the 1978 CPS-SRC election survey, Kuklinski and West (1981) examine two items, one of which is the standard personal retrospective financial item discussed above. The other, though, is decidedly prospective: "Now looking ahead—Do you think that a year from now you will be better off financially, or worse off, or just about the same as now?" The finding is that pocketbook voting took place, but just in the Senate races and just prospectively. As they put it, "expectations about financial well-being during the upcoming year are significantly and strongly related to support for Senate candidates" (442). This result is noteworthy, for it hints that prior economic voting models have been improperly specified. However, for several reasons, it has limitations: (1) only one survey is examined; (2) presidential elections, where economic voting has appeared more important, are not treated; and (3) no questions measuring collective economic judgments are included.

These shortcomings are met in Fiorina (1981), with his investigation of the CPR-SRC surveys from 1974 and 1976. He contends that the vote is determined by future expectations as well as by past experiences. To tap future economic expectations, the following question from the 1974 survey is used: "Do you think that the problems of inflation and unemployment would be handled better by the Democrats, by the Republicans, or about the same by both?" (In the 1976 survey, a related item was administered twice, for the inflation problem and again for the unemployment problem.) Following a thoughtful specification and estimation of voting models for congressional and presidential elections, he finds that these future economic expectations obviously influence the vote. Although this takes steps beyond the Kuklinski and West (1981) work, it still has difficulties. First, uncertainty exists concerning the actual future-orientation of the survey question. Note that the wording uses the conditional tense ("would be handled"), instead of the future tense ("will be handled"). Second, the item seeks a "complex" rather than a "simple" evaluation. Possibly, simple evaluations of the economy by itself, without reference to parties, would produce more modest results. Third, like Kuklinski and West (1981), the Fiorina (1981) results rest on just a few items. Moreover, the questions fail to explore the various time lags (e.g., the last year, the last five years), or time leads (e.g., next year, the next five years), thus preventing a complete estimation of the economic voting time frame.

While this American survey work must be regarded as preliminary, it hints at the presence of a significant, but neglected, prospective component to economic evaluation and incumbent support in U.S. elections. Obviously, additional relevant U.S. survey data would be helpful.

Additional Data: 1984 Surveys of Consumer Attitudes

Since 1946, the Survey Research Center of the University of Michigan, under the Monitoring Economic Change Program, has regularly conducted national Surveys of Consumer Attitudes, asking about family finances, general business conditions, unemployment, interest rates, prices, and buying decisions on consumer goods. Important as they are, these data have seldom been utilized by political scientists, because of the paucity of items on politics. But for two of the Surveys of Consumer Attitudes going into the 1984 elections (those of January and July), items on political preferences were administered.[1] Hence, this rich vein can now be mined. Some of the items, however, are clearly not very useful for economic voting studies, e.g., "During the next 12 months, what do you think are the chances that you will buy one of these recreational vehicles (such as a van, motorhome, camper, or trailer)?"

Items like this, which measure very specific consumer behaviors, were omitted from analysis. Nevertheless, a variety of valuable items remains. The three most-investigated dimensions of economic voting have multiple measures: retrospective-prospective, personal-collective, and simple-complex (see chap. 3). Out of these, I chose questions that stress the global, as opposed to the particular, economic condition; e.g., "Would you say that at the present time business conditions are better or worse than they were a year ago?" The item measures the retrospective, collective, and simple evaluation dimensions. Further, it asks about the global performance of the economy, rather than about a specific component such as unemployment. (Indeed, the item functions empirically as an index of more specific economic evaluations; in particular, a battery of less global items, including ones on prices, unemployment, and interest rates, has a high relationship with it, $R = .6$.) Such global items serve as the basis for the data analysis and are presented below.

The Time Frame of Presidential Pocketbook Voting

To commence, I examine presidential vote intention, where pocketbook voting has been found to have a small, but persistent, place. Do presidential voters who are financially distressed locate their difficulties in the past or in the future? When forming evaluations of their personal circumstances, are they retrospective or prospective? The Surveys of Consumer Attitudes offer some answers, for each has four standard items on personal finances, differing merely with respect to the time frame under evaluation:

1. "We are interested in how people are getting along financially these days. Would you say that you (and your family living there) are better off or worse off financially than you were a year ago?"
2. "Now thinking back 5 years, would you say you (and your family living there) are better off or worse off financially now than you were 5 years ago?"
3. "Now looking ahead—do you think that a year from now you (and your family living there) will be better off financially, or worse off, or just about the same as now?"
4. "And 5 years from now, do you expect that you (and your family living there) will be better off financially, worse off, or just about the same as now?"

Each of these items yields a modest correlation with presidential vote choice (Republican candidate versus Democratic candidate). For instance, the correlations (r) from the July, 1984, survey are .20, .18, .20, and .16, respectively. These findings imply that voters who see themselves as financially better off are more likely to support President Reagan. What is more intriguing, they also point up the perils of surveys that measure personal finances with only one question. That is to say, since the magnitudes of the correlations are about equal, any particular theory on timing—retrospective or prospective—appears equally supported, depending on the items administered. Obviously, a more comprehensive model is preferred, one that includes comparison of several benchmarks on the time line.

The intent here is not to elaborate a full-blown voting model of the American electorate, an impossible task given the scarcity of noneconomic measures in the surveys. Still, the specification of critical control variables is imperative. Besides the usual SES variables (income, race, gender), party identification must be included. However, the standard seven-point, cross-sectional survey measure of party identification has been under criticism (see Fiorina 1981, chap. 5). The worry is that this measure is not exogenous, but rather endogenous. To the extent that party identification as traditionally measured is, indeed, merely the product of current events—such as economic conditions—then its presence in a multiple regression equation next to economic perception measures robs the latter of some explanatory power. At least three possible tools exist, each of which aims to create an exogenous measure: (1) an instrumental party identification variable; (2) a three-point party identification variable; (3) a lagged party identification variable. Because of the scarcity of satisfactory instruments, the first could not be employed; however, the second and third possibilities could.

Party identification was elicited by the standard CPS item ("Generally speaking, do you usually think of yourself as . . . ?); but the respondents were only permitted to select from the three basic categories: Republican, Independent, or Democrat. (In other words, respondents were not asked to distinguish their attachments in terms of "strong" or "weak," adjectives which might be subject to more short-term change than basic party label.) Further, a subset of respondents was actually interviewed in both waves, forming a panel survey. Thus, vote choice in July, 1984, could be related to party identification in January (PID[t-1]), instead of the contemporaneous party identification measure (PID[t]). All these considerations suggest this basic model of the presidential vote decision:

$$\text{Vote} = f[\text{personal fin}_{(t \pm n)}, \text{SES}_{(t)}, \text{PID}_{(t-1)}]. \tag{8.1}$$

Estimates for this model, applied to the 1984 presidential vote intention, appear in table 8.1.

With this more comprehensive specification of the time dimension, what happens to the pocketbook voter hypothesis? The estimates support the generally confirmed finding that personal financial situation exercises a statistically significant effect on presidential vote. However, that significance comes not from the standard retrospective item on personal finances (R_1). Rather, it comes from the prospective item (F_1), which asks respondents to evaluate their economic well-being "a year from now." Apparently, voters who believed that they would be better off in the future were more likely to vote for incumbent Reagan. It seems that, to the extent presidential pocketbook voting took place in 1984, it was actually prospective.

Before accepting this conclusion, it is useful to set aside some methodological objections. Is the absence of significant retrospective effects due to high multicollinearity among the economic variables? Is the presence of a prospective effect due to the peculiar placement of the item in the survey instrument? Is the prospective estimate more unreliable, due to measurement uncertainties? Is the presence of a prospective effect unique to this particular item, in this particular survey?

With regard to the first, some intercorrelation of the economic variables would be expected, given the continuities in financial fortune that most people experience. Are these linkages so great that any coefficients from an equation containing all four—R_5, R_1, F_1, F_5—would be unreliable? To test this possibility, I regressed each on all the others, e.g., F_5 on F_1, R_1, R_5. In no case does the resulting R^2 exceed .29, which is neither near unity nor the R^2 for the overall model in table 8.1 (Farrar and Glauber 1967). (The test R^2 for R_1, the prime retrospective variable, is only .20.) The multicollinearity argument is not supported.

The second objection raises the possibility, put forward by Sears and Lau (1983), that significant pocketbook effects may be artifactual, a product of placing the economic and political items too close together. Such proximate placement, so the argument goes, sensitizes respondents, causing them to rationalize their political preferences in order to make them more congruent with their economic perceptions. To forestall this difficulty in the construction of the questionnaire, the political items were located at some distance from the economic items, (i.e., about seventy questions and subquestions separated the two groups). Moreover, as already discussed (chap. 3), direct evidence from Michigan election surveys suggests that this suspected artifact is not actually present. For these reasons, I conclude that this significant prospective pocketbook vote is not attributable to item placement.

The third concern is that a prospective estimate might be more unreliable

TABLE 8.1   Pocketbook Voting in the
1984 Presidential Election (OLS)

Independent Variables	Coefficients
Personal finances	
Five years ago (R_5)	.04
One year ago (R_1)	.03
Next year (F_1)	.10*
Next five years (F_5)	.00
Controls	
Party ID$_{(t-1)}$	.32*
Income	.02
Race	$-.16$
Gender	$-.08$
Constant	.49*
R^2	.41

*Indicates statistical significance at .05 (one-tail, $t > 1.65$).

Note: The dependent variable is presidential vote intention (July, 1984, Survey of Consumer Attitudes), 1 = Republican candidate, 2 = Democratic candidate. The independent variables of personal finances—R_5, R_1, F_1, F_5—all have codes of 1 = better, 2 = same, 3 = worse. Party identification is a lagged variable from the January survey, coded 1 = Republican, 2 = Independent, 3 = Democrat. For the SES variables, income is a 10-point scale from low to high, race is dichotomized into 1 = white and 0 = other, gender is coded 0 = female and 1 = male. For these estimates, $N = 190$.

than a retrospective one, since prospective measures exhibit more variance (as a result of uncertainties the respondent faces in projecting into the future). This theoretical concern is not realized here, because in fact all the personal economic variables manifest almost identical variance. The standard deviations are as follows: $R_5 = .79$, $R_1 = .77$, $F_1 = .64$, $F_5 = .71$.

What about the fourth contention, focusing on item construction and sampling? These possibilities are explored by looking at the performance of an alternative pocketbook item in a different survey. Respondents were asked the following questions, which seek an evaluation of the course of family income adjusted for the blows of inflation:

1. "During the last year or two, would you say that your (family) income went up more than prices, went up about the same as prices, or went up less than prices?"
2. "How about the next year or two—do you expect that your (family) income will go up more than prices will go up, about the same, or less than prices will go up?"

The first item is an alternate, retrospective measure of personal financial situation, looking at "the last year or two." Suppose these economic variables are simply substituted for the economic variables in table 8.1 and the equation estimated for the larger January survey. The results appear in table 8.2. Again, even with these substitutions, prospective concerns about family economics are significant, while the retrospective concerns are not.

The foregoing methodological search sustains the initial conclusion that, to the extent direct presidential pocketbook voting matters at all, it is more likely to be motivated by future concerns. Further, these prospective evaluations have survived tests on the rival retrospective hypotheses, whereas earlier studies simply assumed the retrospective model.[2]

This does not mean, though, that simple retrospective economic judgments play no part in the presidential voter's calculus. Past personal economic perceptions do manage to exert some influence over the vote, but they take an indirect route. Judgments about our economic future are colored by our economic history. Past economic circumstances, as we recall them, shape our financial hopes, which can then tug at us in the voting booth. Such a relationship (as constrained by the data at hand) is sketched in the arrow diagram of figure 8.1. Economic experiences from five years ago (R_5) influence the evaluation of last year's financial situation (R_1), which in turn molds next year's prospects (F_1), themselves leading to a long-run, five-year assessment (F_5). The general functional form of the relationship, then, is

$$Et = f(E_{t-1}, E_{t-2}, E_{t-3}, \ldots , E_{t-k}), \qquad (8.2)$$

where an economic evaluation (E) for a certain time (t) is determined by evaluations for an earlier time. Besides past economic variables, the expectation is that each evaluation is also formed by other central factors; i.e., place in the social structure (SES) and general political orientation (party identification). The following set of equations suggests itself for estimation of the relations in figure 8.1:

$$R_1 = aR_5 + \text{control variables} \tag{8.3}$$

$$F_1 = bR_1 + bR_5 + \text{control variables} \tag{8.4}$$

$$F_5 = cR_1 + cR_5 + cF_1 + \text{control variables} \tag{8.5}$$

where R_1 = personal financial situation one year ago; R_5 = personal financial situation five years ago; F_1 = personal financial situation next year; F_5 = personal financial situation in five years; control variables = income, race, gender, and party identification, as measured in table 8.1.

TABLE 8.2   **Alternate Estimates of Pocketbook Voting in the 1984 Presidential Election (OLS)**

Independent Variables	Coefficients
Price-adjusted income	
One to two years ago	.00
Next one to two years	.03*
Controls	
Party ID	.37*
Income	−.02*
Race	−.08
Gender	−.05
Constant	.75*
R^2	.54

*Indicates statistical significance at .05 (one-tail, $t > 1.65$).

Note: The dependent variable is presidential vote intention (January, 1984, Survey of Consumer Attitudes), 1 = Republican candidate, 2 = Democratic candidate. The economic independent variables are price-adjusted income the last year or two, and price-adjusted income the next year or two (both measured from more = 1 to less = 5). Party identification is measured contemporaneously and is coded as with table 8.1; the SES variables are also coded as in table 8.1. $N = 381$.

Assuming the system of equations is recursive (i.e., one-way causation and uncorrelated error across equations) then OLS estimation is preferred over 2SLS or some other simultaneous equation technique. As is the custom with path analysis, these estimates are standardized and reported as path coefficients in figure 8.1.

First, with regard to the structure of economic thinking, the path model is revealing. The chain of influence is across the economic events that are contiguous over time. Along the time line, each variable is shaped only by its immediate predecessor. That is, the significant paths flow from the evaluation five years ago to one year ago, from one year ago to next year, from next year to the next five years. However, there is no significant transmission of influence along the paths which traverse a greater span of time. Indeed, the path from five years ago to five years from now, a ten-year stretch of personal economic history, registers .00. And the more distant paths, which cover a six-year period—five years ago to next year, last year to five years from now—fall short of statistical significance. These patterns are not surprising (and they essentially repeat themselves in the January survey). They indicate, as one might imagine, that more immediate economic experiences and expectations are more salient for the voter. What is especially valuable about these results is the verisimilitude it gives the survey instrument. That is to say, the different items are able correctly to order economic events along the time dimension, even though the survey respondents have to make their evaluations during one time point.

What about the strength of effects? The personal economics of an earlier time appears capable of exerting a fairly strong influence on later perceptions. The strongest path, beta = .46, is from the financial situation five years ago (R_5) to the current financial situation as compared to a year ago (R_1). Further, the path from an evaluation based on last year (R_1) to an evaluation based on next year (F_1) is moderately strong, beta = .31. This last, explicit link from a retrospective to a prospective judgment forces the question of indirect influences.

According to the path model, simple retrospective economic judgments exercise indirect effects on the presidential vote decision, with next year's prospective judgment acting as a gatekeeper. More specifically, the two retrospective evaluations, R_1 and R_5, have an impact on the prospective evaluation (F_1) through the paths weighted, respectively, .31 and (.46 × .31). This prospective evaluation for next year, in turn, has a direct effect on vote choice (as demonstrated by the equation of table 8.1; further, this direct effect beta = .14). Hence, even though retrospective judgments appear to have no direct effect themselves on vote choice (following table 8.1), these significant indirect influences allow a partial restoration of its importance. While prospective evaluation still seems to have an edge in shaping the vote, the retrospective

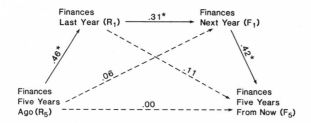

Fig. 8.1. Path model of personal economic evaluations. These path estimates are from the July, 1984, Survey of Consumer Attitudes (see eqs. 8.3–5). For clarity, paths from the control variables are not reported. The asterisk (*) indicates statistical significance at .05 (t > 1.65). The sample size is from 226 to 238, depending on the equation.

evaluations do manage some roundabout impact. Ignoring these intermediate influences would deny retrospective personal economic considerations a small, but proper, place in the presidential voter's decision-making apparatus.

The Time Frame for Collective Economic Voting

While the American pocketbook voter is sometimes elusive (even nonexistent in congressional elections), collective economic voting is easy to find. If Americans are dissatisfied with the course of the national economy, they have a decided tendency to vote against the incumbent party. In the present surveys, interviewees were asked to make the following evaluation of government and the economy:

1. "As to the economic policy of the government—I mean steps taken to fight inflation or unemployment—would you say the government is doing a good job, only fair, or a poor job?"

This collective economic variable (G) has a good correlation with vote intention (Republican candidate versus Democratic candidate). For instance, using the January survey, $r = .58$ for the presidential race, $r = .44$ for the congressional race.[3] The strength of the association remains, even in the face of potent multivariate controls. In table 8.3, this variable is regressed on 1984 presidential and congressional vote intentions, along with party identification and SES variables.

Observe that this collective evaluation (G) is "complex"; that is, the economy and government are assessed together. Further, the respondent is asked for a global assessment, covering both inflation and unemployment.

Thus, this government economic policy item stands as something of a lightning rod measure for political and economic dissatisfactions. It appears to exert a good deal of force on vote intention. In terms of a linear probability approach, its slope suggests that a group of presidential voters who changed their policy evaluation from "good" (1) to "poor" (5) would have a 44 percent lower chance of voting for the incumbent. Further, the impact bears comparison to that of party identification. For instance, the standardized slope coefficient for the variable is .32, over half that for party identification at .55. Moreover, the effects are judged symmetric, with a "good" evaluation having the same magnitude of impact as a "poor" evaluation.

This symmetric effect, and the impressive effects of the government economic policy variable in general, are sustained with a logit analysis (see table 8.4). The effect of government economic policy is highly significant (both the policy dummies have coefficients that are over four times their standard errors), and that effect is balanced, with a "good" evaluation of economic policy having about the same impact as a "poor" evaluation (the logit "partial R" for $G_1 = .181$, and for $G_2 = -.195$). When these partials are compared to those of party identification, again the indication is that policy evaluation has an impact at least half that of party identification (i.e., for ID_1, the "partial R" = .37, for $ID_2 = .31$).

The potent, pivotal role of this policy variable in economic voting makes

TABLE 8.3 Government Economic Policy Evaluation as a Determinant of 1984 Vote Intention (OLS)

Independent Variables	Dependent Variables	
	Presidential Vote Intention	Congressional Vote Intention
Government economic policy (G)	.11*	.06*
Controls		
Party ID	.31*	.37*
Income	−.02*	−.01*
Race	−.01	.01
Gender	−.03	.04
Constant	.61*	.64*
R^2	.61	.55
N	382	398

*Indicates statistical significance at .05 (one-tail, t > 1.65).

Note: The data are from the January, 1984, Survey of Consumer Attitudes. The dependent variables and the control variables are measured as in table 8.2. The economic variable of government economic policy is coded from "good job" = 1, to "poor job" = 5.

perfect sense when one considers how simple collective economic dissatisfactions must convert themselves into a vote choice. Dissatisfaction over performance of the economy has to lead to dissatisfaction over national government policy before government support is altered. Put another way, if there is no mediating link between the economy and the government, then there is no reason to expect a vote switch. Hence, vote probabilities are changed by evaluation of government economic policy (G), which itself is molded by simple collective economic evaluations (SCEs):

$$G = f(SCEs) \qquad (8.6)$$

The question now becomes the timing of influence from these simple collective evaluations. The expectation would be that both retrospective and prospective judgments would have an impact. In these surveys, the following three simple collective economic questions, basically alike except for the time frame, were posed:

1. "Now turning to business conditions in the country as a whole—do you think that during the next 12 months we'll have good times financially, or bad times, or what?"

TABLE 8.4   Determinants of 1984 Presidential Vote Intention (Logit)

Independent Variables	Coefficients
Good economic policy (G_1)	2.05[a] (.47)
Poor economic policy (G_2)	−2.69[a] (.58)
Republican party ID (ID_1)	4.88[a] (.57)
Independent (ID_2)	3.08[a] (.43)
Income (N)	−0.63 (.38)
Race (R)	−0.18 (.72)
Gender (G)	0.16 (.37)
Constant	−1.81[a] (.42)
Pseudo-R	.76
N	382

Codes: Presidential vote intention (January, 1984), income, race, and gender are measured as in table 8.2. G_1 = dummy for "good job" on government economic policy; G_2 = dummy for "poor job" on government economic policy; ID_1, ID_2 = party identification dummies, respectively, for Republicans and Independents; the figures in parentheses are standard errors.

[a]At least twice the size of the standard error.

2. "Would you say that at the present time business conditions are better or worse than they were a year ago?"

3. "Looking ahead, which would you say is more likely—that in the country as a whole we'll have continuous good times during the next 5 years or so, or that we will have periods of widespread unemployment or depression, or what?"

The questions measure overall business conditions for the past year (R'_1), next year (F'_1), and the next five years (F'_5). The variable for government economic policy (G) is an ideal receiver of these time-dependent influences, for it is an evaluation whose wording fixes it in the present, instead of biasing it toward the future or the past. In other words, it seeks a judgment about how government "is doing," rather than how it "did" or "will do." Theoretically, then, this contemporaneous judgment could be built up equally of past experiences and future expectations. In table 8.5, this government economic policy

TABLE 8.5   Prospective and Retrospective Determinants of Government Economic Policy Evaluation, G (OLS), 1984

Economic Variables	Coefficients (January)	Coefficients (July)	
		No. 1[a]	No. 2[b]
Economy next 5 years (F'_5)	0.16*	.23*	.09*
Economy next year (F'_1)	0.14*	.13*	.05
Economy last year (R'_1)	0.14*	.17*	.09*
Controls			
Party ID	0.45*	.36*	−.03
Income	−0.02	−.06*	−.06*
Race	−0.34*	.10	.42
Gender	−0.09	.00	.00
Presidential approval			.58*
Constant	1.31*	.94*	.54
R^2	.29	.31	.52
N	521	213	210

*Indicates statistical significance at .05 (one-tail, $t > 1.65$).

Note: The data are from the January and July, 1984, Surveys of Consumer Attitudes. The dependent variable of government economic policy evaluation (G) is coded as in table 8.3, as are the control variables. The presidential approval variable is coded from 1 = strongly approve of handling job, to 5 = strongly disapprove. The economic variables are coded as follows: R'_1 = business conditions last year (from 1 = better to 5 = worse); F'_1 = business conditions next twelve months (1–5 scale: good times, good with qualifications, pro-con, bad with qualifications, bad times); F'_5 = business conditions next twelve months (1–5 scale, good times to bad times).

[a]Equation specification without "presidential approval" variable.

[b]Equation specification with "presidential approval" variable.

variable (G) is estimated as a function of the SCEs (R'_1, F'_1, F'_5), plus the usual controls. (Note that party identification is always from time t. Apparently, once this variable is measured with a three-category code, lagging it over a six-month period fails to produce further exogeneity. For instance, the January, (t-1), and July, (t), party identification measures have the same correlation, .35, with the July government economic policy variable. Moreover, reliance on the time t measures allows more comparability across the January and July surveys.)

The findings show that simple collective economic evaluations influence this overall "complex" evaluation of government economic policy. Specifically, when voters perceive national business conditions are better, they are significantly more likely to give a praiseworthy evaluation of government economic policy. In the formation of this evaluation, what has more impact, the prospective or the retrospective economic conditions? First, it should be noted that both are important. And a strict comparison of coefficients from a one-year retrospective evaluation (R'_1) and a one-year prospective evaluation (F'_1) indicates that they have about equal impact, i.e., the slope coefficient for either of these items (each scored 1–5) is about .14. But this comparison ignores the significant coefficient from the five-year prospective evaluation, which is of at least that magnitude. Thus, it seems safe to conclude that in terms of immediate effects *prospective evaluations weigh as heavily as retrospective*. (This conclusion is bolstered by the logit analysis in table 8.6.)

TABLE 8.6   Prospective and Retrospective Determinants of Government Economic Policy Evaluation, G (Polychotomous Logit), 1984

Economic Variables	January Coefficients (January)			July Coefficients (July)		
Economy next 5 years (F'_5)	.28[a]	(.06)	[.13]	.37[a]	(.10)	[.17]
Economy next year (F'_1)	.22[a]	(.07)	[.09]	.32[a]	(.10)	[.14]
Economy last year (R'_1)	.27[a]	(.07)	[.12]	.23[a]	(.10)	[.09]
Controls						
Party ID	.52[a]	(.11)		.47[a]	(.18)	
Income	−.06	(.03)		−.12[a]	(.05)	
Race	.48[a]	(.23)		−.28	(.42)	
Gender	.21	(.18)		.10	(.30)	
Pseudo-R		.36			.37	

Note: The data and variables are from table 8.5. The polychotomous logit estimates are from SAS. Figures in parentheses are the standard errors. Figures in brackets are "partial Rs." The constant estimates are not reported. On sample sizes, see table 8.5.

[a]Coefficient at least twice as large as its standard error.

Where Do These Prospective Judgments Originate?

The notion that voters are genuinely prospective has met with some resistance. Are these judgments about the future "real," or are they mere "rationalizations"? (See Conover, Feldman, and Knight 1987.) Different models to account for the origins of these expectations have been proposed (see Alt 1979; Lucas and Sargent 1981; Maddock and Carter 1982). A major concern is that any observed link between prospective evaluation and the vote reflects mere partisan rationalization. In these national consumer surveys, party identification has been variously measured and carefully controlled for. The prospective economic evaluations manage a statistically independent effect. Nevertheless, one might argue that the controls are imperfect and that rationalization continues to creep in. Specifically, "liking" Reagan leads voters to support administration economic policy (just because they "like" Reagan, not because they really approve of the policy). The Reagan bias, the argument continues, cannot be fully removed by simply controlling on party identification. So as a test, a general "presidential approval" item was added to the equation (see specification no. 2, for July in table 8.5). This presidential popularity variable should soak up any rationalization. Besides, it should pick up other possible determinants, such as "leadership qualities" or "foreign policy handling." *In this highly controlled model, the prospective effect is understandably reduced. However, it is still significant and of equal magnitude to the retrospective effect.* The rationalization hypothesis fails to be confirmed.

Another criticism is that prospective evaluations are no more than "projections" of retrospective evaluations. These data certainly do indicate that retrospective economic judgments strongly influence prospective judgments. However, the latter are not totally determined by the former. In the various estimated equations (see table 8.5), prospective judgments always exercise a significant impact on vote intention, even after taking into account retrospective judgments.

Thus, systematic variation exists in economic expectations that has nothing to do with the past, but has a fair amount to do with vote intention. However, it has been contended that the variability in these prospective evaluations is greater, and more full of error, than retrospective ones. By implication, the significant prospective results are unreliable, even a fluke. To test the relative variability of these items, here are the standard deviations: $R'_1 = 1.58$, $F'_1 = 1.66$, $F'_5 = 1.60$ (for July); $R'_1 = 1.42$, $F'_1 = 1.56$, $F'_5 = 1.61$ (for January). One sees that the variation in responses to these items is virtually identical, spatially and temporally. The strength of the prospective effects cannot be dismissed as an artifact of differing variances.

If the prospective evaluations are "real" determinants, then where do they come from? First, they come from retrospective evaluations. Second, they come from campaign promises. While I report evidence on the first, these surveys contain no relevant measures on the second. However, the argument itself is not strained:

A voter, in evaluating parties and candidates, weighs what they say they *will do*, as well as what they *have done*.

Promises, then, are the stuff of these prospective judgments, and future research should incorporate direct measures of candidate *promises*, as well as candidate *performance*.

Jacobson (1988) has recently done relevant work on congressional vote intentions, focusing on the last six weeks of campaigning in the 1986 elections. In addition to his findings on challenger spending, he reports that "economic expectations" significantly influence the vote. Besides the valuable attention the study gives to candidate characteristics, it also indicates the impact of prospective economic evaluations in other electoral contexts. The results offered here, then, can less easily be explained away as peculiar to Reagan and 1984.

What Role Do Retrospective Collective Evaluations Play?

Before arriving at a final conclusion on the relative importance of retrospective and prospective evaluations, indirect effects ought to be taken into account. The arrow diagram in figure 8.2 provides a summary of the links of economic judgments to the vote and to one another. The path coefficients (standardized OLS estimates) are from the following assumed-recursive system of equations:

$$F'_1 = aR'_1 + \text{controls} \tag{8.7}$$

$$F'_5 = bR'_1 + bF'_1 + \text{controls} \tag{8.8}$$

$$G = cR'_1 + cF'_1 + cF'_5 + \text{controls} \tag{8.9}$$

$$V_c = dG + \text{controls} \tag{8.10}$$

$$V_p = eG + \text{controls} \tag{8.11}$$

where F'_1 = business conditions one year from now; F'_5 = business conditions five years from now; R'_1 = business conditions a year ago; G = government economic policy; controls = income, gender, race, and party identification, all measured as for eq. 8.6; V_p = presidential vote choice (Republican or Democrat); V_c = congressional vote choice (Republican or Democrat).

A. January Survey

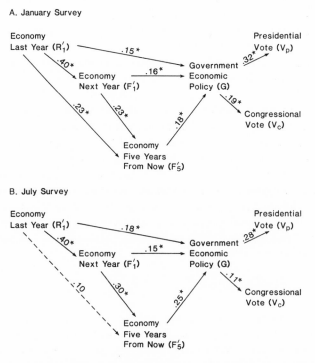

Fig. 8.2.   Path model of collective economic voting, 1984. For clarity, the path estimates (standardized OLS coefficients) from the control variables for each equation—sex, income, race, party identification—are not reported. The asterisk (*) indicates statistical significance at .05 (t > 1.65). The sample size depends on the survey and on the equation. For January, *N* = 521 for the government economic policy (G) equation (eq. 8.9). For July, with the comparable equation, *N* = 213.

The path coefficients show once again the clear, logical bounds between past and present economic evaluations. Note the strong link from one adjacent temporal judgment to the next, e.g., the path from R'_1 to F'_1 is .40, and from F'_1 to F'_5 is .30 (in fig. 8.2B). In this chain, retrospective evaluation is shown to shape prospective evaluation, hence indirectly influencing evaluations of government economy policy (i.e., the path from R'_1 to F'_1 to G, then the path from R'_1 to F'_1 to F'_5 to G). Recollection of how the economy performed helps determine perceptions of how it will perform. If these indirect influences fail to be taken into account, the effect of retrospective evaluations is underestimated. Likewise, the indirect effect of short-run prospective evaluation on long-run prospective evaluation must be considered. That is to say, next year's judgment on business conditions alters the five-year evaluation.

Therefore, indirect effects radiate from both prospective and retrospective centers. And what is particularly interesting, they are or more or less the same strength; i.e., the indirect effect coefficient (IE) of $R'_1 = .09$, while the IE of $F'_1 = .08$. (The first IE is calculated by multiplying through the two significant paths from R'_1 to F'_1 and to F'_5, to G; the second IE comes from multiplying through the single significant path from F'_1 to F'_5 to G. On effects coefficients, see Lewis-Beck and Mohr 1976.) The implication is noteworthy: the overall assessment of the relative importance of prospective and retrospective judgments stays essentially the same, even after including the possibility of these indirect effects. The conclusion, then, is rather firm: *Prospective collective economic evaluations are as important as retrospective collective economic evaluations for the American voter.* Voting models of the U.S. electorate that include only retrospective measures of collective economic evaluations are misspecified and will tend to produce estimates of economic effects that are biased downward.

Summary and Conclusions

What is the time horizon of the American economic voter? Aggregate time series modelers have mostly concluded on theoretical and empirical grounds that it is retrospective. But the nature of that retrospective response is not clear, for the data support many patterns. Survey research offers a unique opportunity here, getting us closer to the individual mechanics of economic voting. Nevertheless, within current survey work, the retrospective economic voter model dominates.

The research at hand has tested, rather than assumed, the retrospective voter model, pitting it against a prospective one. The tests were carried out on new data from the 1984 Surveys of Consumer Attitudes, which include many economic evaluations, tapping the major dimensions that have been previously studied. The findings confirm the importance of retrospective economic voting, particularly at the level of collective evaluations. By now, this is an unremarkable result. However, the impact of prospective evaluations is remarkable. First, presidential pocketbook voting is future-oriented. That is, voters who thought they would be better off financially next year were the ones more likely to support the incumbent president. Second, expectations about the future direction of the whole economy led to decisive alterations in vote intention. Further, these *prospective economic evaluations have an effect at least as strong as that of retrospective evaluations.*

As much as past economic performance, then, it was the promise of the future that gave President Reagan his victory in 1984. Looking at the July survey, 63 percent of the respondents believed that next year would bring the nation unqualified "good times." (Further, 37 percent of this sample actually felt that they themselves would experience financial gains in the next year, as opposed to only 10 percent who felt they would be worse off.) This kind of economic optimism returned Ronald Reagan with a landslide.

A prospective interpretation of the 1984 presidential contest is not beyond dispute. Clearly, critical observers of that race virtually all agree that economic voting—not arms control, Central America, conservatism, the debates, Geraldine Ferraro, religion, or Yuppies—won it for Reagan (Frankovic 1985; Kiewiet and Rivers 1985; Lipset 1985; Norpoth 1985). But just as widely held is the view that this economic voting was retrospective. For instance, in the words of Frankovic (1985, 47), the election "was a referendum . . . particularly on the incumbent's economic performance. A clear majority of the voters saw the economy as better than it had been." Or as Kiewiet and Rivers (1985, 5 and 20) put it, "Mondale lost because the economy was booming, unemployment was falling, inflation was under control and Ronald Reagan was president. . . . [E]conomic conditions of the previous few years are what really matter." The analysis reported herein does show without doubt that retrospective economic evaluations were an important determinant of Reagan support. They also show that prospective economic evaluations had equal force. A look at Reagan's campaign message, read beside other survey data, fills in the prospective argument.

As politicians typically do in campaigns, President Reagan underlined past economic gains. Further, as with other politicians, he spelled out his hopes for the economic future. During a televised speech on the day before the election, he called up an especially bright tomorrow: "All across this shining land we are hoping together. . . . We can say to the world and pledge to our children: America's best days lie ahead" (*New York Times*, November 6, 1984, 12Y). The preelection dreams of Bruce Neller, a young salesman from Dayton, were more specific and concrete: "The issue that's important to me is who *will* [italics added] put money in my pocket" (*New York Times*, November 2, 1984, 16). Such hopes about future prosperity help explain the Reagan votes that cannot be accounted for by traditional retrospective theory.

A good example here comes from the voting behavior of Iowa farmers. By the time of the election, Iowa farmers were in the midst of their worst economic crisis since the Great Depression, with over one-quarter of their farms in danger of financial collapse (*Wall Street Journal*, October 5, 1984, 1). And, by a ratio of two to one, when polled they responded that economically matters were worse now than four years ago (Iowa Poll, *Des Moines Register*, November 4, 1984, 5A). A traditional retrospective theory of economic voting would say that these farmers should be strongly pro-Mondale, but they were not. Instead, 64 percent of them declared a vote for Reagan, against just 31 percent for Mondale. Why this great support for Reagan? A persuasive answer is prospective economic voting. These Iowa farmers, when queried about the future of the farm economy, were more likely to feel that Reagan, rather than Mondale, would solve things. Hence, in voting for President Reagan, they ignored their negative retrospective economic evaluation, following instead their favorable prospective assessment.

Certainly, the belief that Reagan would do a better job of running the economy was shared by other Americans. For example, in a CBS/*New York Times* poll, 47 percent of those who were registered voters said Mondale would make the economy worse, compared to just 26 percent who said Reagan would make it worse (*New York Times*, November 4, 1984, 15F). Looking at a number of surveys, William Schneider (*National Journal*, October 29, 1983, 2202) concluded that voters' economic experience could not completely explain their optimism about Reagan's future economic management; as he put it, the "results suggest that positive views of Reagan's economic programs are based on hope." *In other words, President Reagan was supported not only because of what he delivered economically, but because of what he promised to deliver.*

This conclusion runs counter to traditional retrospective economic voting theory. However, it fits well with the scattered U.S. findings on prospective economic voting. And it is certainly in accord with the strong prospective findings reported earlier from the Western European surveys. *Economic voters in these nations do act retrospectively, just as Key (and Downs) have described. However, they also respond to a purely prospective component of economic evaluation.* In more general studies of issue voting in American elections, the importance of prospective evaluation is coming to be appreciated (Miller and Wattenberg 1985). As has been noted by Fiorina (1981, 15), "the mix of behavior between retrospective and prospective voting is an important question to address." If these results are to be believed, prospective evaluation is as important as retrospective evaluation. Perhaps the old-fashioned textbook notion, that elections offer voters a prospective choice, is not so bad. In fact, Magruder (1942, 438) was speaking with some accuracy when he claimed that party politics involves "organizing the people who hold similar views to support candidates who promise to carry out these views if elected." These promises, at least in their economic guise, are strong stimuli for the electorates in these Western democracies. Indeed, these promises shape the citizen's prospective economic evaluations, which in turn are decisive at the polls.

NOTES

1. Under support of National Science Foundation Grant SES 83-06020 (awarded to the author), four political items were included in the January and July, 1984, Michigan

Survey Research Center Surveys of Consumer Attitudes, which are carried out on a monthly basis by the Monitoring Economic Change Program, directed by Richard Curtin. These individuals and institutions deserve thanks for their valuable aid, but they shoulder no responsibility for the interpretation I have given the data. The four items concern presidential vote intention, congressional vote intention, presidential approval, and party identification. The presidential vote question was, ''If the presidential election were held tomorrow, would you vote for the Republican candidate, the Democratic candidate, or what?'' A count of those who answered ''Republican'' or ''Democrat'' yields $N = 418$ for the January survey. Part of this sample was systematically reinterviewed in July, for a comparable $N = 220$. The two samples each seem correctly to mirror the political choices of the American voter in the 1984 contest. According to the January sample, Reagan would win with 58 percent; the July sample gives an estimate of 62 percent. Reagan's actual portion was 59 percent of the popular vote, which indicates that the survey estimates can be quite accurate, easily within the boundaries of usual sampling error.

The supplemented set of consumer surveys provides especially useful data, since almost all public opinion studies on economic voting have been based on the NES surveys. One exception is Sigelman and Tsai (1981), who use NORC General Social Survey data.

2. Under certain conditions, the prospective presidential pocketbook effects could be stronger. If the voter perceives ''a close race'' for the presidency, he or she appears more likely to vote on the basis of personal economic expectations, according to Henderson's (1986) interaction analysis. By his argument, when voters see the race as close, they believe their vote has more weight; therefore, they are more willing to act on financial self-interest.

3. It is interesting to compare, in a rough way, economic voting effects in the United States and the Western European nations under study. Unfortunately, precise comparison is impossible because the items are different, but the simple correlations are instructive. When this simple correlation of .58 between government economic policy evaluation and presidential vote is put against the correlations of collective economic evaluations and incumbent support in the 1983 and 1984 Euro-Barometers, it is exceeded only in Britain (see table 3.4). Of course, this finding reinforces the general argument that number of parties in the ruling coalition influences the strength of economic voting (see chap. 7).

Chapter 9

The Political Business Cycle and Hyperopic Voters: Resolving a Paradox

> Few British governments have spurned the charms of a pre-election boom, which is why the economy has a history of post-election busts. (*Economist*, October 26, 1985, 20)

> I would expect some easing of austerity as the [1986] election approaches. (Jacques Plassard, French economist, *Wall Street Journal*, July 2, 1985, 34)

> For incumbents, a little better performance before November at the cost of a lot of trouble later still appears to be a good deal. (Paul McCracken, former chairman, Council of Economic Advisers)

Citizens in these leading Western democracies—Britain, France, Germany, Italy, Spain, the United States—are staunch economic voters. When the economy falters, they can be depended upon to vote against the government. Thus, assuming it seeks reelection, the government should pursue policies that ensure the timely arrival of economic prosperity. Indeed, if the government regularly gives special stimulation to the economy around elections, then a political business cycle is created. That is, the usual boom-and-bust pattern of the economy is influenced by elections, during which politicians try to buy votes. Does this kind of political business cycle really exist? Research on the question is voluminous, at least for the United States case, and it mostly points to the same negative conclusion.

After discussing two earlier comparative studies—that of Nordhaus (1975) and of Tufte (1978)—and considering the results of later research, I carry out my own analysis, finding that there is no electoral cycle of economic outcomes, either retrospective or prospective, in any of these nations. Finally, I try to resolve the paradox of null findings on a political business cycle coupled with strong positive findings on economic voting. The answer appears to lie with the uncertainties of economic policy making and, especially, with the hyperopic character of much economic voting.

Traditional Political Business Cycle Theory

A "traditional" political business cycle would seem expected, given a citizenry of economic voters. The assumptions of traditional theory, for government and for voters, might be stated as follows (cf. Alt and Chrystal 1983, 104):

With regard to government:
1. Government seeks reelection.
2. Government can alter the economy.
3. Government alters the economy for electoral gain.
With regard to voters:
1. Voters seek economic benefits.
2. Voters reward the government for economic benefits.
3. Voters are myopic.

These assumptions are especially clear in the pioneering work of Nordhaus (1975), who still guides much contemporary research. He makes the following key assumptions, which are specifications of the above.

With regard to government:
1. Government only wants to win elections.
2. Government can set the unemployment rate at any desired level.
3. Government selects economic policies that maximize votes at the upcoming election.
With regard to voters:
1. Voters prefer stable prices and low unemployment.
2. Voters are ignorant of the macroeconomic trade-off between inflation and unemployment (as shown in the Phillips curve).
3. Voters evaluate economic policies retrospectively, with memory decaying over the electoral period.

These assumptions lead to a hypothesized political business cycle of the following form (Nordhaus 1975, 184):

Immediately after an election the victor will raise unemployment to some relatively high level in order to combat inflation. As elections approach, the unemployment rate will be lowered until, on election eve, the unemployment rate will be lowered to the purely myopic point.

In testing for the presence of such a cycle, Nordhaus simplifies the hypothesis as follows: " During an electoral period of length X, the unemployment rate should rise in the first X/2 years and fall in the second X/2 years" (185).

The hypothesis is tested on annual data from 1947 to 1972, for nine countries—Australia, Canada, France, Germany, Japan, New Zealand, Sweden, Britain, the United States. In general, it is not confirmed. Evidence for this political business cycle is found in only three of the countries. Let us look at the data for the countries that both Nordhaus and the present study examine—Britain, France, Germany, the United States (see table 9.1).

Of these four nations, Britain offers the clearest case of no cycle. That is, the unemployment rate is equally likely to fall or rise, either before or after the election. The French case, although not as sharp, also fails to reveal the cycle. With regard to the German case, there is some support, at least in the preelection period. The United States offers the clearest confirmation. Before elections, unemployment is always falling, never rising; after elections, unemployment almost always rises, only once falling.

But even these American results are not as strong as one might like, for several evident reasons: (1) there are observations on only five elections; (2) the differences are categorical (i.e., rising versus falling) rather than numeric, so precise magnitudes are not known; and (3) the before and after dichotomy for the entire electoral period is crude. Moreover, an implication of Nordhaus's assumptions is that this political business cycle would yield a suboptimal amount of inflation (Nordhaus 1975, 178). Nevertheless, Germany and the United States, his two best cases, actually had the lowest inflation rates of any of the countries studied. *Overall, then, while Nordhaus has contributed much to the theory of the political business cycle, his data do not unequivocally support his theory in any of these countries.*

At least with regard to the United States, perhaps the most influential propolitical business cycle study has been that of Tufte (1978). He argues the

TABLE 9.1   Unemployment Patterns before and after Elections,
Four Nations, Nordhaus Study

	Britain	France	Germany	U.S.
Unemployment rate				
Before elections				
Rising	2	2	0	0
Falling[a]	2	2	5	5
After elections				
Rising[a]	3	4	2	4
Falling	3	1	2	1
Fits hypothesis[a]	5	6	7	9
Does not fit hypothesis	5	3	2	1

Source: Nordhaus 1975, p. 186.
[a]Indicates conformity with the Nordhaus hypothesis.

existence of an ''electoral-economic cycle [that] breeds a lurching, stop-and-go economy the world over'' (143). According to him, the cause is obvious enough: ''Incumbent politicians desire re-election and they believe that a booming preelection economy will help achieve it'' (5). To back up this assertion, Tufte systematically amasses a wealth of data, most of it on the United States case. The principal evidence comes from tracking the course of two macroeconomic variables—disposable income and unemployment—across the electoral calendar. For example, examining the American data from 1947 to 1976 (but excluding the Eisenhower years) he finds that real disposable income growth increased in eight of the eleven election years—73 percent, compared to only two of the ten nonelection years—20 percent (15). With regard to the second variable, he says that unemployment usually reaches its low point in the November of a presidential election year (19). That is, the unemployment rate a year or so on either side of the presidential election averages one or two percentage points higher, respectively—again excluding the Eisenhower years (21). How do incumbents bring about these election-targeted macroeconomic changes? Mostly, they do it by manipulating the amount and timing of government transfers, e.g., Social Security payments, veterans benefits (Tufte 1978, chap. 2).

In Tufte's view, an electoral-economic cycle operates in other democracies besides the United States. As evidence, he looks at the real disposable income growth rate and the election pattern for twenty-seven democracies during the period 1961–72 (Tufte 1978, 11–13). The finding is that, taking the twenty-seven nations as a whole, real disposable income growth increased in 64 percent of all election years, compared to 49 percent of all the nonelection

TABLE 9.2 Elections and Acceleration of Real Disposable Income, Five Nations, 1961–72, Tufte Study

| Nation | Percentage of Years When Real Disposable Income Increased | | | |
	Election Year	N	Nonelection Year	N
Britain	67%	3	38%	8
France	60	5	33	6
Germany	33	3	38	8
Italy	33	3	50	8
United States	83	6	40	5

Source: Tufte 1975, 13.

years. Examining the countries individually, nineteen of the twenty-seven showed something of an electoral-economic cycle. In table 9.2 are Tufte's figures for the countries which are also of interest here. On the basis of these results, it appears there might be a political business cycle in Britain and France, as well as in the United States. For Germany and Italy, it looks as if there is no cycle.

How convincing is Tufte's evidence? Not very. Here are some major problems, looking first at the United States case. He says that real disposable income is the key element in the electoral-economic cycle (Tufte 1978, 29). But, this proposition receives its main support from his exclusion of the Eisenhower years. When the disposable income figures for these years are included, the picture changes considerably. For the period 1947–76, Eisenhower years included, one finds real disposable income accelerated in eight of fifteen election years—53 percent, compared to five of fourteen nonelection years—36 percent (15). Clearly, with these Eisenhower years included, the difference between election and nonelection years is greatly diminished, to the point where it would not attain statistical significance at conventional levels. Similarly with the supposed four-year unemployment cycle, the Eisenhower years do not fit the generalization (19–21). Further, eyeballing the plots of the unemployment rates for the remaining presidential elections, it appears that the November election year values for 1964, 1968, and 1972 are merely part of downward trends that the unemployment variable experienced across the time period, mostly as a result of Great Society and Vietnam War spending. For 1976, the November value seems to begin a downward trend and in any case is not the lowest value over the preceding twelve months. The theory of the four-year unemployment-electoral cycle in the United States, then, rests on shaky empirical ground.

The comparative evidence is also weak. Recall that in the twenty-seven democracies studied, real disposable income accelerated in 64 percent of the election years, $N = 90$, as compared to 49 percent in the nonelection years, $N = 205$ (Tufte 1978, 11). This difference of 15 percent is small, bordering on statistical insignificance (Weisberg and Bowen 1977, 141). At best, it would imply that the electoral cycle is a mild influence on income, which is largely determined by other forces. Further, this small difference rests on a small number of years (9–12) in each country, in a purposefully selected sample. Thus, it is reasonable to think that slight alterations in the choice of years or nations could make the results still less favorable.

Last, but not least, Tufte's findings on the countries of interest here contradict the findings of Nordhaus (see the summary in table 9.3). They only agree on a political business cycle for the United States, and are at odds on Britain, France, and Germany.

TABLE 9.3   Comparison of the Tufte and Nordhaus Evidence on Political Business Cycles in Five Nations

Country	Did Tufte Find Cycle?	Did Nordhaus Find Cycle?	Do the Results Agree?
Britain	Yes	No	No
France	Yes	No	No
Germany	No	Yes	No
Italy	No	—	—
United States	Yes	Yes	Yes

Later Evidence

The pathbreaking efforts of Nordhaus and Tufte certainly developed political business cycle studies. Nevertheless, their empirical work does not give much support to the idea of a traditional political business cycle in these Western democracies. Further, more elaborate country-specific efforts have failed to produce positive results. (On the United States, see MacRae 1977; McCallum 1978; on Britain, see Chrystal and Alt 1981b; on France, see Monroe 1980.) In his careful comparative study of seventeen OECD nations, 1948–75, Paldam (1981b) likewise uncovers no evidence for what he calls the Nordhaus-MacRae model. Other recent work has reached the same conclusion (Alt and Chrystal 1983, 125; Brown and Stein 1982; Winters et al. 1981). Keech and Pak (1988, 1) summarize these sentiments well: "We do not believe that political business cycles of the Nordhaus or Tufte type exist as a systematic, regular and important phenomenon."[1]

My analysis, which estimates a general political business cycle model for these five countries—Britain, France, Germany, Italy, the United States—comes to the same conclusion. To begin, recall the argument that the unemployment rate (U_t) reaches its low point in the election year (E_t), then increases in the year after (E_{t+1}). Further, over the post–World War II period, the annual unemployment rate has tended to follow a linear trend (T_t). Such considerations initially suggest these electoral-unemployment models for estimation (proposed as separate equations to avoid the inevitable problems of multicollinearity between E_t and E_{t+1}):

$$U_t = b_0 + b_1 E_t + b_2 T_t + e \qquad (9.1)$$

$$U_t = a_0 + a_1(E_{t+1}) + a_2 T_t + e \qquad (9.2)$$

where U_t = the annual unemployment rate; E_t = an electoral cycle dummy variable coded 1 for election year, 0 otherwise; E_{t+1} = an electoral cycle dummy variable coded 1 for the year after an election, 0 otherwise; T_t = a linear counter variable for years, 1,2, . . . , n; e = error; b_0, b_1, b_2, a_0, a_1, a_2 = the parameters to be estimated.

The electoral-unemployment cycle notion can be simply stated:

Incumbents reduce the unemployment rate before an election and allow it to increase after the election.

These, then, are the relevant hypotheses: $b_1 < 0$; $a_1 > 0$.

I estimated these equations for Britain, France, Germany, Italy, and the United States for the years 1958 to 1983 (see table 9.4). The results could hardly be less supportive of the traditional political business cycle idea. None of the coefficients is close to statistical significance. Further, the signs follow a more or less random pattern, e.g., three of one, two of another, for each election dummy. (The null findings continue if a third dummy, E_{t-1}, is ana-

TABLE 9.4   Estimates (OLS) for an Election-Unemployment Cycle in Five Nations, 1958–83

	Britain	France	Germany	Italy	United States
	$U_t = b_0 + b_1E_t + b_2T_t + e$				
b0	−0.64	−0.57	−0.28	3.60*	4.21*
	(−0.93)	(−1.48)	(−0.46)	(10.07)	(7.06)
b1	−0.11	0.04	−0.08	0.31	−0.22
	(−0.15)	(0.10)	(−0.12)	(0.79)	(−0.34)
b2	0.31*	0.28*	0.19*	0.17*	0.13*
	(7.15)	(12.04)	(5.01)	(7.66)	(3.39)
R^2	.69	.86	.53	.72	.34
	$U_t = a_0 + a_1(E_{t+1}) + a_2T_t + e$				
a0	−0.48	−0.61	−0.24	3.68*	4.24*
	(−0.69)	(−1.68)	(0.39)	(10.36)	(7.28)
a1	−0.69	0.30	−0.14	0.02	−0.43
	(−0.91)	(0.73)	(−0.21)	(0.06)	(−0.66)
a2	0.31*	0.28*	0.19*	0.17*	0.13*
	(7.20)	(12.16)	(5.02)	(7.52)	(3.45)
R^2	.70	.87	.53	.71	.35

*Indicates statistical significance at .05 (one-tail, $t > 1.71$).

Note: The data on annual unemployment rates, 1958–83, are taken from OECD sources. U_t = annual unemployment rate; E_t = election year dummy scored 1 if election year and 0 otherwise (for the European nations this tags parliamentary elections, for the United States, presidential); E_{t+1} = a postelection year dummy; T = a counter variable for years, 1, 2, . . . , n; N = 25; the figures in parentheses are t-ratios.

lyzed.) In fact, not a single country follows the overall expectation of lowered unemployment going into the election ($b_1 < 0$) and increased unemployment after the election ($a_1 > 0$). (It is worth noting that multicollinearity between E_t and T_t has not produced these null results, which are just as pronounced if the trend variables are excluded.)

Thus, my analysis fails to uncover an electoral-unemployment cycle in any of these nations. However, there may be another macroeconomic target for vote-seeking politicians—inflation. Tufte (1978, 60) notes that "deflationary policies are less likely to be pursued in election years than in years without elections." Also, Nordhaus (1975, 178) argues that the incumbent "percentage of votes is a decreasing function of both the unemployment and inflation rates." Therefore, one might expect an electoral-inflation cycle, with a drop in the inflation rate going into the election, followed by an increase in the inflation rate in the postelection year (assuming the Phillips curve). This suggests models similar to the above, where the inflation rate is a function of the electoral calendar, plus a long-term trend variable.

The model estimates are in table 9.5. Again, no political business cycle can be detected. In the election year equations, two coefficients have the expected sign ($-$), three the unexpected ($+$). Further, none of these coeffi-

TABLE 9.5   Estimates (OLS) for an Election-Inflation Cycle in Five Nations, 1958–83

	Britain	France	Germany	Italy	United States
		($I_t = b_0 + b_1E_t + b_2T_t + e$)			
b0	0.94	3.07*	1.77*	−1.04	0.17
	(0.49)	(2.17)	(3.07)	(−0.66)	(0.17)
b1	−1.57	1.27	−0.39	0.27	0.10
	(−0.77)	(0.87)	(−0.61)	(0.15)	(0.09)
b2	0.55*	0.31*	0.15*	0.73*	0.36*
	(4.60)	(3.59)	(4.03)	(7.43)	(5.61)
R^2	.48	.37	.41	.71	.58
		[$I_t = a_0 + a_1E_{(t+1)} + a_2T_t + e$]			
a0	−0.35	3.20*	1.43*	−1.21	0.21
	(−0.19)	(2.34)	(2.44)	(−0.78)	(0.20)
a1	3.23	1.43	0.86	1.03	−0.04
	(1.57)	(0.93)	(1.42)	(0.60)	(−0.03)
a2	0.56*	0.30*	0.15*	0.73*	0.36*
	(4.85)	(3.51)	(4.22)	(7.51)	(5.60)
R^2	.52	.37	.45	.71	.58

Note: The data are from the *International Financial Statistics Yearbook,* International Monetary Fund, 1984; I_t = the annual inflation rate; the other variables and statistics are as in table 9.4.

cients is close to statistical significance (at .05, one-tail, t > 1.71). With regard
to the postelection coefficients, while four of the five are in the expected
direction (+), they all fail the statistical significance test. A reliable electoral-
inflation cycle simply does not emerge from these data, regardless of country.

In the search for a traditional political business cycle, the guiding idea is
that the incumbent brings about electorally timed systematic changes in macroeconomic outcomes—unemployment, inflation, growth. The last has yet to be
analyzed here. The key variable in Tufte's electoral-economic cycle was
growth rate in real disposable income. (And, at one point, his substitute, the
growth rate of real GNP [Tufte 1978, 65–66].) The global measures of national
income (or product) have some advantage over the unemployment and inflation
measures. First, they are more comprehensive, including the direct and indirect effects of these more specific measures. Second, virtually all economic
policies of government would receive some weight in such a variable. According to simple political business cycle theory, growth should accelerate in
election years. What about the postelection years? Following Tufte (1978, 24),
the expectation would be that this subsequent year, election-free and with low
electoral stakes, has a lowered rate of growth. Taking off from the earlier
models, similar equations suggest themselves.

The estimates are reported in table 9.6. Still the evidence for a political

TABLE 9.6 Estimates (OLS) for an Election–Economic Growth Cycle in Five Nations, 1958–83

	Britain	France	Germany	Italy	United States
		$(G_t = b_0 + b_1E_t + b_2T_t + e)$			
b0	0.03*	0.07*	0.07*	0.07*	0.03*
	(3.85)	(8.87)	(6.12)	(7.05)	(3.13)
b1	0.005	−0.003	0.01	0.006	0.02
	(0.50)	(−0.40)	(1.11)	(0.56)	(1.47)
b2	−0.001	−0.002*	−0.003*	−0.002*	−0.001
	(−1.67)	(−3.70)	(−3.56)	(−3.78)	(−0.94)
R^2	.12	.37	.36	.40	.12
		$[G_t = a_0 + a_1E_{(t+1)} + a_2T_t + e]$			
a0	0.04*	0.07*	0.08*	0.07*	0.03*
	(4.33)	(9.01)	(6.31)	(7.21)	(3.27)
a1	−0.01	0.000	−0.01	0.01	0.02
	(−1.04)	(0.01)	(−0.96)	(1.10)	(1.54)
a2	−0.001*	−.002*	−0.003*	−0.002*	−0.001
	(−1.75)	(3.67)	(−3.48)	(−3.90)	(−1.06)
R^2	.15	.37	.35	.42	.13

Note: The data are from the OECD; G_t = the annual growth rate of the GDP; the
other variables and statistics are as in table 9.4.

business cycle is unconvincing. The governments in power do not manage to give the economy a special boost around election time. None of the coefficients for E_t is statistically significant at .05. Looking at the signs for the (E_{t+1}) coefficients, only two are in the correct direction, and none is statistically significant. With regard to specific countries, only two, Germany and Britain, even exhibit the proper pattern of signs (i.e., $+b_1$ and $-a_1$), and the t-ratios are weak in both instances. For the United States, the t-ratio for the election-year dummy falls short of statistical significance, and the postelection coefficient for the United States is perversely signed. Especially given the context of the other findings, the case for an electoral–growth rate cycle in the United States remains weak.

Does This Mean No Kind of
Political Business Cycle Exists?

In the foregoing, I have related the electoral calendar to three macroeconomic outcomes—unemployment, inflation, growth—in five leading Western democracies. The investigation produced negligible evidence of a traditional political business cycle in these countries, as have virtually all other studies on the subject. However, it would be premature to conclude that absolutely no species of electoral-economic connection is possible. The political business cycle models tested thus far could be called *incumbency-oriented* models of macroeconomic outcomes. However, another type of model is *party-oriented*. A party-oriented model argues that different ruling parties lead to different macroeconomic outcomes. For example, a ruling Socialist party, with a working-class constituency, might set a lower unemployment rate than a ruling Conservative party, with a middle-class constituency.

Such models, interesting as they are, must be clearly distinguished from the traditional political business cycle idea. The kernel of that idea, captured in the incumbency-oriented models, is to put the economy in time with the electoral calendar in order to maximize votes. Timing is everything (so we tend to look for economic spikes on a time line in order to confirm the theory). With the party-oriented models, in contrast, the economy changes after an election in response to the ideological pursuits of the ruling party. Ideology is everything (so we tend to look for stair-step shifts from one election period to the next in order to confirm the theory). It is perhaps confusing to treat these party-oriented models as political business cycle models, and Tufte (1978, chap. 4), for one, does not. Turning to the evidence, the conclusions on such models are in dispute (Alesina and Sachs 1988; Alt 1985; Beck 1982; Chappell and Keech 1986; Havrilesky 1987; Hibbs 1977, 1987). While further work may clearly establish the importance of this party-oriented pattern, it is not really a lively concern here. Rather, what is sought is evidence of vote-maximizing behavior of incumbents around election time, in response to the heavy economic voting visible in these electorates.

The analyses in tables 9.4–.6 have given clear indication that central macroeconomic outcomes are insensitive to the electoral cycle. However, these null results still leave open the possibility that incumbents did manage to alter economic policy for electoral purposes. In fact, it has been suggested that political business cycle scholars might examine incumbency-oriented models with economic policy *instruments* as the dependent variable, rather than macroeconomic *outcomes* themselves. Because these economic policy instruments are more directly under the control of the incumbent, their organized manipulation in order to gain votes might be more readily detected. This line of inquiry, promising as it seems, has not borne much fruit. In the United States, the adjustment of fiscal instruments has generally been found unrelated to the electoral calendar (Berry and Lowery 1987; Kamlet and Mowery 1987; Lowery 1985; for an exception, see Swank 1988). More particularly, the swings in the full-employment deficit do not show a connection to the electoral cycle (Golden and Poterba 1980). Interestingly, Keech and Pak (1988) conclude that veterans benefits were once subject to an electoral cycle, but are no longer. With regard to U.S. monetary policies, they also appear independent of preelection political influence (Beck 1980; Beck 1987; Kane 1980). Thus, across this range of instruments, there seems to be little election-based policy manipulation.

Still, while traces of systematic policy or performance change along the lines of a traditional political business cycle may be absent, few would deny that *politicians may try* to engineer one.[2] The idea certainly has a good deal of symbolic importance. Around election time, it is easy to observe some politicians seeking votes in exchange for economic favors to the constituency. In the United States, at least since the New Deal, select federal programs have been targeted for their electoral impact (Wright 1974). Before elections, American presidents have yielded to industry pressures for tariff protection from foreign competition. The timely announcement of new government projects and grants to the district is de rigueur for legislators seeking reelection (Anagnoson 1982). The "liberal hour" of congressional appropriations around election time has become well documented (Hibbing 1984; Kiewiet and McCubbins 1985). The doling out of patronage and key administrative appointments is often made with an eye to the electoral calendar. These commonplace gestures are important, for they undoubtedly net votes, and they show constituents that their representatives are working for them (on Britain and the United States, see Cain, Frejohn, and Fiorina 1987). Nevertheless, added together, *these gestures apparently do not manage to deflect significantly the trajectory of the macroeconomy around elections.*

Why No Traditional Political
Business Cycle? Uncertainty

This research has not uncovered a traditional political business cycle (PBC). More particularly, it appears that in these leading democracies, politicians of the governing party (or parties) do not provide a special, vote-getting boost to the economy before the election. Hence the paradox: *if voters are moved by economic benefits and governments want to win reelection, then why no PBC?* There are at least two reasons. The first has to do with the actual timing of economic manipulations. The second involves the underlying assumption of a myopic electorate.

A strong reason why the data reveal no traditional political business cycle has to do with the delivery time of economic programs and policies. Government is uncertain about when the economic benefits will arrive. According to the analysis of previous chapters, voters respond to real (or perceived real) collective economic change. To bring about short-run change in the level of economic activity, government must operate fiscal and monetary tools, inevitably with some imprecision (Tobin 1980). Here are American examples: a tax cut targeted for a certain time may be delayed in Congress; an authorized rise in Social Security may arrive after the election; the Federal Reserve Board may swing from overly tight money to overly loose money; or a pump-priming public works proposal may take hold after the economy is already on the upswing.

Samuelson (1976, 359) gives a telling example of the last, where the cure for recession is building post offices. It is worth quoting at length:

> Plans must be made; blueprints drawn; land acquired by purchase and court condemnation; existing buildings razed; and then new structures and roads constructed. All this may take five or more years; and, at the least, half of this time may elapse before any sizeable amount of money will get spent on labor and materials. Suppose the recession turns out to last a year at most, followed by two years of steady advance. Then, just in the third year, when the economy may have gone all the way from too little demand to too much demand, there will suddenly come onto the market the government spending intended to help a recession.

Because of uncertainty, then, vote-seeking politicians cannot count on a preelection macroeconomic bull's-eye. In aiming for such a bull's-eye, the risk of the benefits reaching the voters too early or too late would be unacceptably high. Instead, then, they pursue economic policies with an eye to the business cycle, rather than the electoral cycle. Of course, this does not mean that they ignore the electorate. That is, they still wish to buy votes. However, in order to accomplish this, policies of economic optimization must be followed. *Politicians who want to win try more or less continuously to provide economic good times.* This is necessary, first, because of the uncertainties over when the good times will actually be delivered; and, second, because of the ranging vision of the economic voter.

Why No Traditional PBC? Hyperopic Voters

Traditional PBC models assume, implicitly or explicitly, that voters are myopic. Specifically, the assumption is that economic voters are hindsighted, with rapidly decaying memory. They vote retrospectively, paying most attention to economic performance in the year of the election and caring little about what happens after. Given this state of mind, it is possible for government to exploit the electorate, e.g., decrease unemployment before an election knowing it will have to increase it after (in order to fight the coming inflation).

The individual-level evidence reported here, as well as elsewhere, certainly demonstrates the presence of such retrospective voting. In each of these nations, retrospective evaluations of national economic performance significantly influence incumbent support. For example, when German citizens felt that government policies had damaged the economy over the past year, they were less likely to declare a vote for the ruling coalition. However, in addition, the economic voting in these countries was discovered to have a strong prospective component. For example, among Germans who believed that government policies over the next year were going to damage the economy, there was a lower probability of incumbent voting.

What are the implications of prospective voting for a PBC? Perhaps traditional models have been misspecified. If voters are paying attention to the economic future, there may be an "election-promise" cycle, rather than an "election-performance" one. In fact, Paldam (1981b, 298–99) makes such a suggestion after finding that growth and inflation rise in the second and third postelection years, respectively. Because voters have memory, promises are not forgotten, and so must be acted on. With these data, *I explored the possibility of a "promise-induced" business cycle appearing two or three years after the election (see table 9.7). However, for none of these macroeconomic indicators—unemployment, inflation, growth—was a significant blip uncovered.* Prospective economic voting, then, does not appear to bring about its own special electoral rhythm.

Individual-level economic voting, either retrospective or prospective, does not manage to generate a national-level PBC counterpart. Why? The answer lies with the relative weight voters appear to give the two types of economic evaluation. The many coefficients previously reported permit the following conclusion: prospective economic evaluations shift incumbent vote probabilities about as much as retrospective economic evaluations do (and these equal effects are orthogonal). Take an example. Suppose a group of voters is pleased with past economic performance, raising their proincumbent vote probability, $+.20$. But suppose they are also concerned over the economic future, lowering their proincumbent vote probability, $-.20$. Then to win this group of voters, the government cannot rest on its past laurels; it must

TABLE 9.7   Estimates (OLS) for a Postelection "Promise" Cycle of Unemployment, Inflation, Growth, in Five Nations, 1958–83

	Britain	France	Germany	Italy	United States
	A. Unemployment Rate $(U_t = b_0 + b_1 E_{[t+n]} + b_2 T_t + e)$				
b0	−0.73	−0.53	−0.36	3.67*	4.12*
	(−1.06)	(−1.40)	(−0.57)	(10.32)	(6.83)
b1	0.26	−0.08	0.23	0.06	0.12
	(0.36)	(−0.22)	(0.31)	(0.18)	(0.18)
b2	0.31*	0.28*	0.20*	0.17*	0.13*
	(7.14)	(12.07)	(5.05)	(7.49)	(3.40)
R^2	.69	.86	.53	.71	.33
	B. Inflation Rate $(I_t = b_0 + b_1 E_{[t+n]} + b_2 T_t + e)$				
b0	0.31	3.95*	1.84*	−0.79	−0.02
	(0.16)	(2.85)	(3.01)	(−0.51)	(−0.02)
b1	0.98	−1.52	−0.41	−0.62	0.71
	(0.48)	(−1.09)	(−0.57)	(−0.40)	(0.66)
b2	0.55*	0.30*	0.14*	0.73*	0.36*
	(4.53)	(3.57)	(3.85)	(7.48)	(5.68)
R^2	.48	.38	.41	.71	.59
	C. GDP Growth Rate $(G_t = b_0 + b_1 E_{[t+n]} + b_2 T_t + e)$				
b0	0.04*	0.06*	0.08*	0.07*	4.45*
	(4.15)	(8.72)	(6.65)	(7.43)	(4.13)
b1	−0.01	0.003	−0.02	−0.004	−1.97
	(−0.55)	(0.35)	(−1.51)	(−0.38)	(−1.75)
b2	−0.001	−0.002*	−0.003*	−0.002*	−0.07
	(−1.64)	(−3.68)	(−3.70)	(−3.79)	(−1.08)
R^2	.12	.37	.39	.39	.15

Note: The data, the definition of the statistics, and the dependent variables are the same as in tables 9.5–7. The postelection "promise" dummy is $E_{(t+n)}$, where $1 =$ two or more years postelection (i.e., scored so as not to include the election year itself, nor the year on either side); $0 =$ otherwise.

alter future expectations. That is, it must deliver convincing promises, as well as solid performance.

Economic voters are harder for government to exploit at election time than previously thought. These voters have a *hyperopic*, as well as a *myopic*, side. They weigh what economic benefits they expect to receive after the election, as well as what economic benefits they have received going into the election. They are likely to balance the benefits of a preelection boom with the costs of a possible postelection bust. When they enter the voting booth, knowledge of this potential trade-off makes them immune to the temptations of an election-induced prosperity. *When voters have foresight, as well as hindsight, the government cannot simply stand on a good economic record. It must also promise a bright economic future.*

Faced with voters who are looking backward and forward on the economic time horizon, a vote-maximizing government must eschew a traditional political business cycle. Voters hold government accountable for economic performance and promise across the entire term, not just across the election campaign. (Remember that today's promise soon becomes the standard for tomorrow's performance.) Hence, wise ("rational") ruling parties are always running for reelection, aiming for optimal economic policies, regardless of the calendar.

Summary and Conclusions

The notion that politicians alter the economy around election time in order to gain votes is intriguing. But the comparative evidence here fails to support a traditional business cycle model. In particular, key macroeconomic outcomes—unemployment, inflation, GDP—do not appear to vary (retrospectively or prospectively) with the electoral calendars of Britain, France, Germany, Italy, or the United States.

This appears paradoxical. The electorates of these nations are dedicated economic voters, and their rulers presumably seek reelection; however, the expected PBC is absent. Resolution is achieved when two things are considered. First, even if the government pursued a strategy of economic stimulation attuned to the electoral calendar, the many uncertainties of timely policy delivery would tend to scatter the ballot effects of the effort. Second, governments actually do not have much incentive to pursue economic manipulations targeted for the election year, because of the time perspective of economic voters. That is, they make prospective as well as retrospective evaluations, which means that politicians will be held accountable not only for what they did do, but also for what they will do. These two conditions, which run against traditional notions of economic policy precision and myopic voters, require that vote-maximizing politicians almost constantly offer economic rewards, thus effacing any cyclical behavior.

NOTES

1. As with any theory that is heavily researched, it is inevitable that some contrary findings will emerge. (For instance, virtually all aggregate time series studies of economic voting establish a link between economics and elections; but, for an exception, see Stigler 1973.) With regard to traditional political business cycle theory, there are a few possible exceptions to the usual null findings. For instance, Haynes and Stone (1987) manage, through the application of spectral analysis to United States data, to find a fourth-year spike in the election quarter. And Allen, Sulock, and Sabo (1986), while failing to find a general cycle, find something for U.S. presidents who are reelected. Finally, all the work considered here refers to cycles at the national level. For Italy, another cycle has been uncovered, with elections tied to local administration budget policies (Brosio, Ferrero, and Santagata 1982).
2. Of course, perhaps incumbents do not even try to alter the macroeconomy, but rather simply benefit from its upswing. In other words, by lucky coincidence the incumbent reaps the credit for good economic performance, and thus the votes. This is an implication from Kiewiet and Rivers (1985), who observe that Reagan's 1984 reelection was optimally timed in terms of the business cycle (while for Carter in 1980, the timing was economically very suboptimal).

Part 4   Conclusion

Chapter 10

Economics and Elections: An Inventory

When you think economics, think elections; When you think elections, think economics. (Tufte 1978, 65)

What can be concluded about the relationship between economics and elections? A number of worthwhile propositions now seem well established. I list the central ones below. Always, the geographic focus is on the Western democracies under investigation—Britain, France, Germany, Italy, Spain, and the United States. These conclusions, distilled from the evidence offered in the foregoing pages, are grouped according to substantive findings, theoretical implications, and research design issues. To facilitate scholarly exchange, I state them as succinctly as possible. The presentation format is stylized: a question (Q) is posed, an answer (A) given, and a clarification (C) made.

Issues of Substance

Q1. Does economics influence elections?

A1. Yes. If economic conditions worsen (improve), citizens are more (less) likely to vote against the incumbent party (or party coalition).

C1. Macroeconomic indicators virtually always register a statistically significant effect in the numerous aggregate time series popularity or vote functions constructed for these nations. Furthermore, individual-level survey-based voting models for these nations consistently demonstrate statistically significant effects from evaluations of economic performance and policy.

Q2. Does economics operate on these citizens through the pocketbook?

A2. Only a little.

C2. Very few citizens are motivated to vote against the incumbent simply because they see their financial situation has deteriorated. In election surveys from these six nations, retrospective personal economic circumstance (no matter how it is measured) virtually always fails to register statistically significant main effects on legislative vote. (An exception is U.S. presidential elections, where a mild effect appears, but that may well be more prospective than retrospective.)

Q3. Practically speaking, does this really mean that the pocketbook never influences these voters?

A3. No.

C3. Under special circumstances pocketbook considerations can have somewhat more effect. When voters attribute responsibility for their economic plight to the government (rather than, say, to themselves), they are more likely to vote against that government. However, the net effect of this interaction is limited in at least two important ways. First, in the United States, very few citizens consciously blame government for their personal financial circumstance. Second, in Western Europe, this attribution effect is transmitted to the vote only indirectly, through its influence on collective economic performance evaluations. Such indirect transmission greatly weakens its practical influence.

Q4. How do economic evaluations affect voters, if not through the pocketbook?

A4. Basically, the economic voter looks at the nation.

C4. That is, evaluations of collective economic performance and policy move the voter. In particular, in each of these nations retrospective and prospective evaluations of government economic management significantly influenced incumbent support. Also, beyond these cognitive evaluations, an affective component of collective economic evaluation appears to exert a significant impact on the vote.

Q5. Is economic voting asymmetric, with "punishment" for bad times, but no "reward" for good times?

A5. No.

C5. Voters in these Western democracies are not one sided, responding only to economic downturn. Instead, they are at least as likely to vote for the incumbent when they perceive good performance, as they are to vote against when they perceive decline.

Q6. How strong an electoral influence do these economic evaluations exercise on individual voters?

A6. Economic evaluations have at least a moderately strong influence on individual voters in legislative elections. In general, for these Western European nations, changes in economic evaluations have more of an impact than do changes in social cleavages (such as religiosity and class), but less of an impact than Left-Right ideological identification. Similarly for the United States, economics has more of an impact than SES variables, but less of an impact than party identification.

C6. When economic evaluations change, the probability of a vote for the incumbent shifts most in Britain and least in Italy. Indeed, in Britain (and

Spain) economic changes have a larger effect even than ideology. Only in Italy do changing social cleavages have more of an effect than changing economic evaluations.

Q7. How strong an electoral influence do these economic evaluations exercise on electoral outcomes for the nation as a whole?

A7. Shifting economic evaluations can make or break incumbents in a reelection bid. That is, individual shifts in economic evaluations can add up to a nontrivial shift in the overall election results.

C7. From one election to the next, rather modest shifts in the percentage of voters who see worsening economic conditions can easily cost the incumbent from 3 to 5 percent of the total popular vote in a parliamentary election in these Western European nations.

Q8. In the voter's calculus, how permanent is the place occupied by economics?

A8. Generally, it appears to have been an enduring factor in post–World War II legislative elections.

C8. Indirect evidence from time series analyses (of Britain, France, Italy, and Germany) shows that economic variables account for electoral change about as well before 1970 as after. Public opinion polls (from France and Britain) across the period show that economic issues have been almost invariably regarded as highly important. Direct survey evidence (from the U.S. congressional elections) shows that economic evaluations were as likely to be statistically significant before 1970 as after.

Q9. How important are economic issues for the individual voter, compared to other, noneconomic, issues?

A9. More important.

C9. Many other issues, besides economics, move Western European electorates. However, none of these other issues correlate as highly or as consistently with vote choice.

Issues of Theory

Q1. Is economic voting retrospective?

A1. Yes, but it is also prospective.

C1. Clearly, voters reward (punish) the incumbent for past economic performance. However, independently, they also reward (punish) the incumbent on the basis of future expectations. These prospective evaluations have about as strong an impact as the retrospective evaluations, in all six nations.

Q2. Is economic voting based on self-interest?

A2. It could be.

C2. The fact that there are negligible pocketbook effects does not in itself dismiss the hypothesis of self-interested voting. A voter who is motivated by a collective evaluation of economic performance, as these voters are, may simply be acting on long-term self-interest. Ruling out the pocketbook voter hypothesis, then, does not automatically turn collective voters into altruists.

Q3. Are economic evaluations exclusively cognitive?

A3. Maybe not.

C3. The implication of the results reported here is that there is an emotional component to economic evaluations, which has an impact on choice independent of the more rational prospective and retrospective calculations. When voters are angry over how government is handling the economy, they tend to declare a vote against the incumbent, regardless of their dispassionate cognitive evaluation of the situation.

Q4. Is there a political business cycle?

A4. No, not in the traditional sense.

C4. Politicians do not appear to engage in special bursts of vote-buying around election time. National economic output does not move to an electoral rhythm. In aggregate time series analyses, no significant pre- or postelection cycles in key macroeconomic outcomes (unemployment, inflation, growth) were uncovered for these countries (Britain, France, Germany, Italy, the United States).

Q5. Given that there are economic voters, why is there no traditional political business cycle?

A5. Mostly, because voters are more or less continuously evaluating economic performance and promises.

C5. Economic voters are motivated by collective judgments, which are prospective as well as retrospective. Hence, voters are not exclusively naive and myopic. In addition, they are sophisticated and hyperopic. They shape their vote intentions according to what will happen to the economy, as well as what has happened. Since these retrospective and prospective components have about equal impact (taking together direct and indirect effects), their net effect is to cancel out the effort and incentive of politicians to manipulate the business cycle around elections. The rational vote-seeking politician is always pursuing a policy of economic optimization.

Q6. Is it necessary to have a different economic voting model for each country?

A6. No.

C6. The process of economic voting is much the same in these nations. That is, the same economic variables operate about the same way, with a similar pattern of statistical significance and coefficients that seldom differ greatly. Moreover, the equations as estimated for each nation generate similar goodness-of-fit statistics (the R^2, the standard error of estimate, and the pseudo-R). Across these Western European democracies, then, the model generalizes rather well.

Q7. Does this mean there is no difference at all in economic voting for these nations?

A7. No. Some difference in the strength of economic voting does appear to exist cross-nationally. The rank-order, from top to bottom, is as follows: Britain, Spain, Germany, France, Italy.

C7. As coalition complexity (measured by the number of parties in the ruling coalition) increases, the strength of economic voting tends to decrease. Thus, one observes the strongest economic voting in Britain, the weakest in Italy. Besides, economic growth appears to be a national contextual factor that positively influences the strength of economic voting. (The ranking of average economic growth rates for these countries perfectly accords with the economic voting strength ranking.)

Q8. Are economic variables necessary for proper specification of voting models in general?

A8. Yes.

C8. Under the imposition of rigorous controls, economic variables continue to demonstrate statistical and substantive importance in shaping vote intention. Therefore, when voting models for these electorates exclude economic variables, they commit specification error. Because of the inevitable collinearity, the coefficients for the included variables in such models would be biased.

Q9. Does this mean that economic evaluation ranks with partisan identification as a determinant of choice for the individual voter?

A9. No, but it occupies a middle ground in terms of importance, somewhere between partisan identification and current issues.

C9. Economic evaluations do not have the exogenous (or near-exogenous) status of partisan or ideological identification. Voters seldom have a long-term standing commitment to a particular economic policy, for example. However, they might be said to have a primary, enduring interest in the nation's economic well-being. And in almost every election, economic conditions (good or bad) are high on the agenda. Unlike other issues, those of economics do not come and go, and are not really short-term. It is no accident that successful politicians have come up with the formula, "peace and prosperity." While economic concerns, then, may fall under the rubric of "issue voting," they certainly represent the premier issue set.

Issues of Research Design

Q1. How should economic voting be studied?

A1. The answer to that question depends on whether the analyst wishes primarily to account for individual voter choice or national election outcome.

C1. If the researcher is interested in assessing how economic conditions influence citizens in their vote choice, then individual voters should be systematically investigated, presumably (but not necessarily) in a scientific survey. The problems of measurement error that inevitably ensue are not a counsel to aggregate data; rather, they simply urge better measurement on individuals. (Of course, this might lead to a pooled analysis, joining the better survey measures with aggregate time series.)

Q2. Does this mean that strict aggregate time series models are without value?

A2. Not at all.

C2. If the analyst is interested in accounting for national election outcomes (i.e., overall vote totals), then aggregate time series models might be preferred. For example, they have an indispensable role in making before-the-fact election forecasts. A further use occurs when the researcher is primarily interested in the net overall effects of economics on the national election outcome. That is, the aggregate level of behavior is the focus, rather than the individual level. In this case, total system effects may be approximated as well from the reduced form coefficients in macromodels, as from building upward with individual-level survey-based coefficients.

Q3. In preparing the survey instrument, what kinds of economic items should be emphasized—personal or collective?

A3. Collective.

C3. No matter how measured, the personal retrospective measures of economic conditions seem little related to vote intention (at least in legislative elections). In contrast, collective economic evaluations reliably relate to vote intention.

Q4. Does this mean no pocketbook items whatsoever should be administered?

A4. No.

C4. They would appear useful in U.S. presidential election surveys, especially prospective items. Likewise, one might want to include prospective pocketbook items in Western European surveys, in order to test the possibility of future-oriented personal economic voting in parliamentary elections.

Q5. In administering the survey, how close should the economic items be to the political items?

A5. Unless they are extremely close, it does not seem to make any difference.

C5. In theory, if an economic evaluation item were administered right after (or right before) a political preference item, an artificial increase in the correlation between the two might result. However, in practice, when the items are kept a reasonable distance apart (say ten or so items between them), then this inflation does not occur.

Q6. Which collective items seem more important, those with the "simple" format or those with the "complex" format?

A6. The "complex" items, which ask the respondent to think about the government as well as the economy.

C6. Items that link the words "government" and "economy" crowd out items that just mention "economy," when two such items are paired in multivariate testing. Further, the complex items tend to maintain a high level of substantive and statistical significance, even after extensive controls on other independent variables (in order to rule out, among other things, the possibility of rationalization).

Q7. What, precisely, are the economic conditions that should be mentioned in the construction of these collective survey items?

A7. The items should focus on general evaluations of economic performance and policy.

C7. The economic voter appears to make a global judgment about the economy and acts accordingly. This global evaluation is composed of particular evaluations of factors such as inflation, unemployment, growth, debt, and balance of trade. These components, taken together, essentially determine the global evaluation. The weights of the components are not identical and vary some across countries and across elections.

What Is Next?

I have attempted to summarize plainly my findings on economics and elections in the six leading Western democracies—Britain, France, Germany, Italy, Spain, and the United States. Possible answers to many questions are proposed. However, a good deal remains to be done. Most importantly, we need to know how firm the conclusions are. Will they stand the test of time? Will they stand the test of other researchers? Certain claims seem ripe for challenge: (1) the generally feeble character of the pocketbook vote, (2) the (otherwise) impressive strength of economic evaluations, (3) the stable presence of economic voting across elections, (4) the lack of asymmetric incumbent punishment for economic hard times, (5) the prominence of prospective evaluations, (6) the appearance of an affective component in economic voting, (7) the lack of a political business cycle, (8) the generalization of the economic voting model across nations, and (9) the importance of economic issues, compared to noneconomic issues, in determining the vote choice. The list could be continued. Such challenges may distress this author, but they should certainly further our understanding of a central theme in modern political economy—the relationship of economics and elections.

References

Abelson, Robert P.; Kinder, Donald R.; Peters, Mark D.; and Fiske, Susan T. 1982. Affective and semantic components in political person perception. *Journal of Personality and Social Psychology* 42 (April): 619–30.

Abramowitz, Alan I., and Segal, Jeffrey A. 1986. Determinants of the outcomes of U.S. Senate elections. *Journal of Politics* 48:433–39.

Achen, Christopher H. 1982. *Interpreting and Using Regression.* Beverly Hills: Sage.

Aldrich, John, and Nelson, Forrest. 1986. Probit and logit methods. In *New Tools for Social Scientists: Advances and Applications in Research Methods,* ed. William Berry and Michael S. Lewis-Beck, 115–56. Beverly Hills: Sage.

Alesina, A., and Sachs, J. 1988. Political parties and the business cycle in the United States, 1948–1984. *Journal of Money, Credit, and Banking* 20:63–82.

Alford, Robert R. 1963. *Party and Society: The Anglo-American Democracies.* Chicago: Rand McNally.

Allen, S., Sulock, J., and Sabo, W. 1986. The political business cycle: How significant? *Public Finance Quarterly* 14:107–12.

Alt, James E. 1979. *The Politics of Economic Decline: Economic Management and Political Behavior in Britain since 1964.* New York: Cambridge University Press.

———. 1984. Dealignment and the dynamics of partisanship in Britain. In *Electoral Change in Advanced Industrial Democracies: Realignment or Dealignment?,* ed. Russell J. Dalton, Scott C. Flanagan, and Paul Allen Beck, 298–329. Princeton: Princeton University Press.

———. 1985. Party strategies, world demand, and unemployment: Domestic and international sources of economic activity. *American Political Science Review* 79:1016–40.

Alt, James, and Chrystal, Alec. 1983. *Political Economics.* Berkeley: University of California Press.

Amor Bravo, Elias M. 1985. El ciclo político de los negocios y su referencia al caso español (1976–1985). *Información Comercial Española* (Boletín Semanal), no. 2015 (December 23–29): 4259–68.

———. 1986. Modelos de popularidad espacial en la economía española: una nota. *Información Comercial Española* (Boletín Semanal), no. 2077 (March 23–29): 1057–58.

———. 1987. Modelos político-económicos en España. *Revista del Instituto de Estudios Economicos* (second quarter): 189–213.

Anagnoson, J. Theodore. 1982. Federal grant agencies and congressional election campaigns. *American Journal of Political Science* 26:547–61.

163

Arcelus, F., and Meltzer, A. H. 1975. The effects of aggregate economic variables on congressional elections. *American Political Science Review* 69:1232–40.

Barnes, Samuel H.; Kaase, Max; and Allerbeck, Klause R. 1979. *Political Action: Mass Participation in Five Western Democracies.* Beverly Hills: Sage.

Beck, Morris. 1980. The public sector and economic stabilization. In *The Business Cycle and Public Policy: 1929–1980.* Joint Committee of U.S. Congress. Washington, D.C.: U.S. Government Printing Office.

Beck, Nathaniel. 1982. Parties, administrations and American macroeconomic outcomes. *American Political Science Review* 76:83–94.

———. 1987. Elections and the Fed: Is there a political monetary cycle? *American Journal of Political Science* 31:194–216.

Bellucci, Paolo. 1984. The effect of aggregate economic conditions on the political preferences of the Italian electorate, 1953–1979. *European Journal of Political Research* 12:387–412.

Bellucci, Paolo, and Lewis-Beck, Michael S. 1983. Economics and the vote in Italy: Part II (the individual level). Paper presented at workshop, Institutional Performance in Italy. Conference Group on Italian Politics, June 14–19, Bellagio, Italy.

Benjamin, Roger, and Elkin, Stephen L. 1985. *The Democratic State.* Lawrence: University of Kansas Press.

Berry, William, and Lewis-Beck, Michael S., eds. 1986. *New Tools for Social Scientists: Advances and Applications in Research Methods.* Beverly Hills: Sage.

Berry, William, and Lowery, David. 1987. *Understanding United States Government Growth.* New York: Praeger.

Bishop, George; Oldendick, Robert W.; and Tuchfarber, Alfred. 1984. What must my interest in politics be if I just told you "I don't know?" *Public Opinion Quarterly* 48:510–19.

Bloom, Howard S., and Price, H. Douglas. 1975. Voter response to short-run economic conditions: The asymmetric effect of prosperity and recession. *American Political Science Review* 69:1240–54.

Box, G. E. P., and Jenkins, G. M. 1976. *Time Series Analysis.* San Francisco: Holden-Day.

Brody, Richard, and Sigelman, Lee. 1983. Presidential popularity and presidential elections: An update and an extension. *Public Opinion Quarterly* 47:325–28.

Brody, Richard, and Sniderman, Paul. 1977. From life space to polling place: The relevance of personal concerns for voting behavior. *British Journal of Political Science* 7:337–60.

Brosio, Giorgio; Ferrero, Mario; and Santagata, Walter. 1982. In search of an electoral cycle in local finance: The Italian case. Paper presented at the Conference of the Council for European Studies, April 29–May 1, Washington, D.C.

Brown, Thad, and Stein, A. 1982. The political economy of national elections. *Comparative Politics* 14:479–97.

Brunk, Greg; Caldeira, Greg; and Lewis-Beck, Michael S. 1987. Capitalism, socialism, democracy: An empirical inquiry. *European Journal of Political Research* 15:459–70.

Budge, Ian; Crewe, Ivor; and Fairlie, Dennis. 1976. *Party Identification and Beyond*. London: Wiley.

Butler, David, and Stokes, Donald. 1969. *Political Change in Britain*. New York: St. Martin's Press.

Cain, Bruce; Frejohn, John; and Fiorina, Morris. 1987. *The Personal Vote: Constituency Service and Electoral Independence*. Cambridge: Harvard University Press.

Cameron, David R. 1978. The expansion of the public economy: A comparative analysis. *American Political Science Review* 72:1243–61.

Campbell, Angus; Converse, Philip E.; Miller, Warren E.; and Stokes, Donald E. 1960. *The American Voter*. New York: Wiley and Sons.

Campbell, James E. 1986. Forecasting the 1986 midterm elections to the House of Representatives. *PS* (Winter): 83–87.

Chappell, Henry W., Jr., and Keech, William R. 1985. A new view of political accountability for economic performance. *American Political Science Review* 79 (March): 10–27.

———. 1986. Party differences in macroeconomic policies and outcomes. *American Economic Review, Papers and Proceedings* 76:71–74.

Chrystal, K. Alec, and Alt, James E. 1981a. Some problems in formulating and testing a politico-economic model of the United Kingdom. *Economic Journal* 91:730–36.

Chrystal, K. Alec, and Alt, James E. 1981b. Public sector behavior: The status of the political business cycle. In *Macroeconomic Analysis*, ed., D. Currie, R. Nobay, and D. Peel. London: Croom Helm.

Claggett, William. 1986. A reexamination of the asymmetry hypothesis: Economic expansions, contractions and congressional elections. *Western Political Quarterly* 39:623–33.

Conover, Pamela Johnston. 1985. The impact of group economic interests on political evaluations. *American Politics Quarterly* 13:139–66.

Conover, Pamela Johnston, and Feldman, Stanley. 1986. Emotional reactions to the economy: I'm mad as hell and I'm not going to take it anymore. *American Journal of Political Science* 30 (February): 50–78.

Conover, Pamela Johnston; Feldman, Stanley; and Knight, Kathleen. 1987. The personal and political underpinnings of economic forecasts. *American Journal of Political Science* 31:559–83.

Converse, Philip E. 1964. The nature of belief systems among mass publics. In *Ideology and Discontent*, ed. D. Apter, 202–61. New York: Free Press.

Dalton, Russell J. 1988. *Citizen Politics in Western Democracies*. Chatham, N.J.: Chatham House.

Dalton, Russell J.; Flanagan, Scott; and Beck, Paul Allen, eds. 1984. *Electoral Change in Advanced Industrial Societies: Realignment or Dealignment?* Princeton: Princeton University Press.

Downs, Anthony. 1957. *An Economic Theory of Democracy*. New York: Harper.

Eulau, Heinz, and Lewis-Beck, Michael S., eds. 1985. *Economic Conditions and Electoral Outcomes*. New York: Agathon.

Falter, Jurgen W., and Zintl, Reinhard. 1985. The economic crisis of the 1930's and
the Nazi vote. Paper presented at the annual meeting of the Midwest Political
Science Association, April 19, Chicago.

Farrar, D. E., and Glauber, R. R. 1967. Multicollinearity in regression analysis: The
problem re-visited. *Review of Economics and Statistics* 49:92–107.

Feldman, Stanley. 1982. Economic self-interest and political behavior. *American
Journal of Political Science* 26:446–66.

———. 1985. Economic self-interest and the vote: Evidence and meaning. In *Economic Conditions and Electoral Outcomes: The United States and Western Europe,* ed. Heinz Eulau and Michael S. Lewis-Beck, 144–66. New York: Agathon
Press.

Finkel, Steven E.; Muller, Edward N.; and Seligson, Mitchell A. 1987. Economic
crisis, incumbent performance and regime support. Paper presented at the annual
meeting of the American Political Science Association, August–September, Chicago.

Fiorina, Morris P. 1978. Economic retrospective voting in American national elections: A micro-analysis. *American Journal of Political Science* 22:426–43.

———. 1981. *Retrospective Voting in American National Elections.* New Haven:
Yale University Press.

Fiske, Susan T., and Taylor, Shelley E. 1984. *Social Cognition.* Reading, Mass.:
Addison-Wesley.

Frankovic, Kathleen A. 1985. The 1984 election: The irrelevance of the campaign. *PS*
18:39–47.

Frey, B. S., and Garbers, H. 1972. Der Einfluss wirtschaftlicher Variabler auf die
Popularität der Regierung. *Jahrbücher für Nationalökonomie und Statistik*
186:281–320.

Frey, B. S.; Pommerehne, W. W.; Schneider, F.; and Guy, Gilbert. 1984. Consensus
and dissension among economists: An empirical inquiry. *American Economic
Review, Papers and Proceedings* 74:986–94.

Frey, B. S., and Schneider, Friedrich. 1978. A politico-economic model of the United
Kingdom. *Economic Journal* 88:243–53.

———. 1979. An econometric model with an endogenous government sector. *Public
Choice* 34:29–43.

———. 1980. Popularity functions: The case of the U.S. and West Germany. In
Models of Political Economy, ed. P. Whiteley, 47–84. London, Sage.

Frey, B. S., and Weck, H. 1981. Hat Arbeitslosigkeit den Aufstieg des National-
Sozialismus bewirkt? *Jahrbücher für Nationalökonomie und Statistik* 196:1–31.

Galli, G., ed. 1968. *Il comportamento elettorale in Italia.* Bologna: Societa Editrice il
Mulino.

Galli, G., and Prandi, A. 1970. *Patterns of Political Participation in Italy.* New
Haven: Yale University Press.

Girauld, R. 1980. L'analyse spectrale: théorie et application à l'étude des interactions
politico-économiques. Ph.D. diss. Université de Paris II.

Golden, D., and Poterba, J. 1980. The price of popularity: The political business cycle
reexamined. *American Journal of Political Science* 24:696–714.

Goodhart, C. A. E., and Bhansali, R. J. 1970. Political economy. *Political Studies* 18:43–106.

Goodman, S., and Kramer, G. 1975. Comment on Arcelus and Meltzer, the effect of aggregate economic conditions on congressional elections. *American Political Science Review* 69:1255–65.

Havrilesky, T. 1987. A partisanship theory of fiscal and monetary regimes. *Journal of Money, Credit and Banking* 19:308–25.

Haynes, S., and Stone, J. 1987. Does the political business cycle dominate United States unemployment and inflation? In *Political Business Cycles: The Economics and Politics of Stagflation,* ed. T. Willett. San Francisco: Pacific Institute.

Henderson, Christopher J. 1986. The cost of altruism: New insight to the pocketbook voter. Unpublished. University of Iowa.

Hibbing, John R. 1984. The liberal hour: Electoral pressures and transfer payment voting in the United States Congress. *Journal of Politics* 46:846–65.

Hibbing, John R., and Alford, John R. 1982. Economic conditions and the forgotten side of Congress: A foray into U.S. Senate elections. *British Journal of Political Science* 12:505–13.

Hibbs, Douglas A., Jr., and Fassbender, H., eds. 1981. *Contemporary Political Economy.* Amsterdam: North-Holland.

———. 1982a. On the demand for economic outcomes: Macroeconomic performance and mass political support in the United States, Great Britain and Germany. *Journal of Politics* 44:426–62.

———. 1982b. President Reagan's mandate from the 1980 elections: A shift to the right? *American Politics Quarterly* 10:387–420.

———. 1987. *The American Political Economy.* Cambridge: Harvard University Press.

Hibbs, Douglass A., Jr., and Fassbender, H., eds. 1981. *Contemporary Political Economy.* Amsterdam: North-Holland.

Hibbs, Douglas A., and Vasilatos, Nicholas. 1981. Economics and politics in France: Economic performance and political support for Presidents Pompidou and Giscard d'Estaing. *European Journal of Political Research* 9:133–45.

Inglehart, Ronald. 1977. *Silent Revolution: Changing Values and Political Styles Among Western Publics.* Princeton: Princeton University Press.

———. 1983. The persistence of materialist and postmaterialist value orientations. *European Journal of Political Research* 11:81–82.

———. 1984. The changing structure of political cleavages in Western society. In *Electoral Change in Advanced Industrial Democracies,* ed. R. Dalton, S. Flanagan, and P. A. Beck, 25–69. Princeton: Princeton University Press.

———. 1987. The renaissance of political culture: Central values, political economy and stable democracy. Paper presented at the annual meeting of the American Political Science Association, August-September, Chicago.

Inglehart, Ronald, and Klingemann, Hans. 1976. Party identification, ideological preference and the Left-Right dimension among Western mass publics. In *Party Identification and Beyond,* ed. Ian Budge, Ivor Crewe, and Dennis Fairie, 243–73. London: Wiley.

Jackman, Robert W. 1985. Cross-national statistical research and the study of comparative politics. *American Journal of Political Science* 29:161–82.

———. 1987. The politics of economic growth in the industrial democracies, 1974–80: Leftist strength or North Sea Oil? *Journal of Politics* 49:243–74.

Jackson, John. 1975. Issues, party choices, and presidential votes. *American Journal of Political Science* 19:161–85.

Jacobson, Gary C. 1983. *The Politics of Congressional Elections*. Boston: Little-Brown.

———. 1988. The effects of campaign spending on voting intentions: New evidence from a panel study of the 1986 House elections. Paper presented at the annual meeting of the Midwest Political Science Association, April 14–16, Chicago.

Jacobson, Gary C., and Kernell, Samuel. 1982. Strategy and choice in the 1982 congressional elections. *PS* 15:423–30.

———. 1983. *Strategy and Choice in Congressional Elections*. New Haven: Yale University Press.

Jennings, M. Kent. 1984. The intergenerational transfer of political ideologies in eight Western nations. *European Journal of Political Research* 12:261–76.

Jordan, Nehemiah. 1965. The "asymmetry" of "liking" and "disliking." *Public Opinion Quarterly* 29 (Summer): 315–22.

Kamlet, Mark S., and Mowery, David C. 1987. Influence on executive and congressional budgetary priorities, 1953–1981. *American Political Science Review* 81:155–78.

Kane, Edward. 1980. Politics and Fed policymaking: The more things change, the more they remain the same. *Journal of Monetary Economics* 6:199–212.

Katona, George; Strumpel, B.; and Zahn, E. 1971. *Aspirations and Affluence*. New York: McGraw-Hill.

Keech, William R., and Pak, Kyoungsan, 1988. Electoral cycles and budgetary growth in veterans benefit programs. Paper presented at the Midwest Political Science Association, April 14–16, Chicago.

Kernell, Samuel. 1977. Presidential popularity and negative voting: An alternative explanation of the mid-term congressional decline of the president's party. *American Political Science Review* 71:44–66.

———. 1980. Strategy and ideology: The politics of unemployment and inflation in modern capitalist democracies. Paper presented at the annual meeting of the American Political Science Association, August–September, Washington, D.C.

Key, V. O., Jr. 1966. *The Responsible Electorate*. New York: Vintage.

Kiewiet, D. Roderick. 1983. *Macroeconomics and Micropolitics: The Electoral Effects of Economic Issues*. Chicago: University of Chicago Press.

———. 1981. Policy-oriented voting in response to economic issues. *American Political Science Review* 75:448–59.

Kiewiet, D. Roderick, and McCubbins, Matthew. 1985. Congressional appropriations and the electoral connection. *Journal of Politics* 47:59–82.

Kiewiet, D. Roderick, and Rivers, Douglas. 1984. A retrospective on retrospective voting. *Political Behavior* 6:369–93.

Kiewiet, D. Roderick, and Rivers, Douglas. 1985. The economic basis of Reagan's appeal. In *The New Direction in American Politics*. ed. John Chubb and Paul Peterson, Washington, D.C.: chap. 3, pp. 1–22. Brookings Institution.

Kinder, Donald R., and Kiewiet, D. Roderick. 1979. Economic discontent and political behavior: The role of personal grievances and collective economic judgments in congressional voting. *American Journal of Political Science* 23:495–527.

———. 1981. Sociotropic politics: The American case. *British Journal of Political Science* 11 (April): 129–41.

Kinder, Donald R., and Mebane, Walter R., Jr. 1983. Politics and economics in everyday life. In *The Political Process and Economic Change*, ed. Kristen Monroe, 141–80. New York: Agathon Press.

Kirchgassner, Gebhard. 1974. Ökonometrische Untersuchungen des Einflusses der Wirtschaftslage auf die Popularität der Parteien. *Schweizerische Aeitschrift für Volkswirtschaft und Statistik* 110:409–45.

———. 1976. Rationales Wählerverhalten und optimales Regierungsverhalten, ein Beitrag zur Untersuchung des Zusammenhangs zwischen dem wirtschaftlichen und dem politischen Teilsystem moderner demokratischer Gesellschaften. Ph.D. diss. Universität Konstanz.

———. 1977. Wirtschaftslage und Wählerverhalten, eine empirische Studie für die Bundesrepublik Deuschland von 1971 bis 1976. *Politische Vierteljahresschrift* 18:510–36.

———. 1983. Welche Art der Beziehung herrscht zwischen der objektiven wirtschaftlichen Entwicklung, der Einschätzung der Wirtschaftslage und der Popularität der Parteien: Unabhängigkeit, Scheinunabhängigkeit, Scheinkorrelation oder kausale Beziehung? Eine empirische Untersuchung für die Bundesrepublik Deutschland von 1971 bis 1982. In *Wahlen und Politisches System, Analysen aud Anlass der Bundestagwahl 1980,* ed. M. Kaase and D. Klingemann, 222–56. Opladen: Westdeutscher Verlag.

———. 1985a. Economic conditions and the popularity of West German parties: A survey. Paper presented at the annual meeting of the Midwest Political Science Association, April 19, Chicago.

———. 1985b. Causality testing of the popularity function: An empirical investigation for the Federal Republic of Germany, 1971–1982. *Public Choice* 45:155–73.

———. 1985c. Rationality, causality, and the relation between economic conditions and the popularity of parties. *European Economic Review* 28:1–2.

———. 1986. Economic conditions and the popularity of West German parties: A survey. *European Journal of Political Research* 14:421–39.

Kramer, Gerald H. 1971. Short-term fluctuations in U.S. voting behavior: 1896–1964. *American Political Science Review* 65:131–43.

———. 1983. The ecological fallacy revisited: Aggregate- versus individual-level findings on economics and elections, and sociotropic voting. *American Political Science Review* 77:92–111.

Krasner, Stephen. 1984. Approaches to the state: Alternative conceptions and historical dynamics. *Comparative Politics* 16:223–46.

Kuklinski, James H., and West, Darrell M. 1981. Economic expectations and voting behavior in United States Senate and House elections. *American Political Science Review* 75:436–47.

Lafay, Jean-Dominique. 1973. Comportements politiques et conjoncture économique. Mimeo. Université de Poitiers.

―――. 1977. Les conséquences électorales de la conjoncture économique: essais de prevision chiffree pur mars 1978. *Vie et sciences economiques* 75:1–7.

―――. 1981a. The impact of economic variables on political behavior in France. In *Contemporary Political Economy,* ed. D. Hibbs and J. Fassbender, 137–49. New York: North-Holland.

―――. 1981b. Empirical analysis of politico-economic interaction in East European countries. *Soviet Studies* 33:386–400.

―――. 1985. Important political change and the stability of the popularity function: Before and after the French General Election of 1981. In Eulau and Lewis-Beck 1985, 78–97.

Lafay, Jean-Dominique; Berdot, J. P.; and Giraud, R. 1981. *Popularity Functions and Models for France: Tables of Preliminary Results.* Mimeo. Université de Poitiers.

Lancaster, Thomas. 1985. Economics, democracy, and Spanish elections. In Eulau and Lewis-Beck 1985, 110–24.

Lancaster, Thomas, and Lewis-Beck, Michael S. 1985. Regional voting: The case of Spain. Paper presented at the annual meeting of the Midwest Political Science Association, April, Chicago.

―――. 1986. The Spanish voter: tradition, economics, ideology. *Journal of Politics* 48:648–74.

Lane, Robert. 1962. *Political Ideology.* New York: Free Press.

Lange, Peter, and Garrett, Geoffrey. 1985. The politics of growth: Strategic interaction and economic performance in the advanced industrial democracies, 1974–1980. *Journal of Politics* 47:792–827.

Lecaillon, J. 1980a. *La crisis et l'alternance.* Paris: Cujas.

―――. 1980b. Salaires, chômage et situation politique. *Revue d'économique politique* 5:615–27.

―――. 1981. Popularité des gouvernements et popularité économique. *Consommation:* 17–50.

―――. 1982. *Disparité de revenues et stratégie politique.* Mimeo. Université de Paris I.

Levy, Maurice. 1981. *Economics Deciphered: A Layman's Survival Guide.* New York: Basic Books.

Lewis-Beck, Michael S. 1980. Economic conditions and executive popularity: The French experience. *American Journal of Political Science* 24:306–23.

―――. 1981. The electoral politics of the French peasantry: 1946–1978. *Political Studies* 29:517–36.

―――. 1983. Economics and the French voter: A microanalysis. *Public Opinion Quarterly* 47:347–60.

―――. 1984. France: The stalled electorate. In Dalton, Flanagan, and Beck 1984, 425–48.

―――. 1985a. Un modèle de prévision des élections législative françaises (avec une application pour 1986). *Revue française de science politique* 35:1080–91.

―――. 1985b. Pocketbook voting in U.S. national election studies: Fact or artifact? *American Journal of Political Science* 29:348–56.

―――. 1986a. Les législatives de 1986: nouveau clivage ou restauration? *Politique economique* 3 (June): 31–33.

———. 1986b. Comparative economic voting: Britain, France, Germany, Italy. *American Journal of Political Science* 30:315–46.

———. 1986c. The growth of the contemporary Italian state. Paper presented at the joint CONGRIP–Stato e Mercato conference, The State and Social Regulation in Italy, April 14–18, Bellagio, Italy.

———. 1988. Economics and the American voter: Past, present, future. *Political Behavior* 10, no. 1: 5–21.

Lewis-Beck, Michael S., and Bellucci, Paolo. 1982. Economic influences on legislative elections in multiparty systems: France and Italy. *Political Behavior* 4:93–107.

Lewis-Beck, Michael S., and Mohr, Lawrence B. 1976. Evaluating the effects of independent variables. *Political Methodology* 3:27–47.

Lewis-Beck, Michael S., and Rice, Tom. 1982. Presidential popularity and presidential vote. *Public Opinion Quarterly* 46:534–37.

———. 1984. Forecasting U.S. House elections. *Legislative Studies Quarterly* 9:475–86.

———. 1985a. Are Senate election outcomes predictable? *PS* 18:745–54.

———. 1985b. Government growth in the United States. *Journal of Politics* 47:2–30.

Lewis-Beck, Michael S., and Skalaban, Andrew. 1988. The R-squared: Some straight talk. Paper presented at the annual meeting of the Midwest Political Science Association, April 15, Chicago.

Lewis-Beck, Michael S., and Squire, Peverill. 1988. Transformation of the American state: The New Era-New Deal test. Unpublished.

Lijphart, Arend. 1971. *Class and Religious Voting in European Democracies.* Glasgow: University of Strathclyde.

Lindbeck, Assar. 1976. Stabilization policy in open economics with endogenous politicians. *American Economic Review, Papers and Proceedings* 66:1–19.

Lipset, Seymour Martin. 1960. *Political Man: The Social Bases of Politics.* Garden City: Doubleday.

———. 1964. The changing class structure and contemporary European politics. *Daedalus* 93:271–303.

———. 1985. The elections, the economy and public opinion: 1984. *PS* 18:28–38.

Lipset, Seymour Martin, and Rokkan, Stein, eds. 1967. *Party Systems and Voter Alignments.* New York: Macmillan.

Lowery, David. 1985. The Keynesian and political determinants of unbalanced budgets: U.S. fiscal policy from Eisenhower to Reagan. *American Journal of Political Science* 29:428–60.

Lucas, Robert E., Jr., and Sargent, Thomas J. 1981. *Rational Expectations: Econometric Practice.* Minneapolis: University of Minnesota Press.

McCallum, B. T. 1978. The political business cycle: An empirical test. *Southern Economic Journal* 44:504–15.

MacRae, D. C. 1977. A political model of the business cycle. *Journal of Political Economy* 85:239–63.

Maddock, R., and Carter, M. 1982. A child's guide to rational expectations. *Journal of Economic Literature* 20:39–51.

Magruder, Frank Abbott. 1942. *American Government.* Boston: Allyn and Bacon.

Markus, Gregory. 1988. The impact of personal and national economic conditions on the presidential vote: A pooled cross-sectional analysis. *American Journal of Political Science* 32:137–54.

Markus, Gregory, and Converse, Philip. 1979. A dynamic simultaneous equation model of electoral choice. *American Political Science Review* 73:1055–70.

Miller, Arthur H., and Wattenberg, Martin P. 1985. Throwing the rascals out: Policy and performance evaluations of presidential candidates, 1952–1980. *American Political Science Review* 79:359–72.

Miller, W. L., and Mackie, M. 1973. The electoral cycle and the asymmetry of government and opposition popularity: An alternative model of the relationship between economic conditions and political popularity. *Political Studies* 21:263–79.

Monroe, Kristen R. 1978. Economic influences on presidential popularity. *Public Opinion Quarterly* 42:360–69.

———. 1979. Economic analysis of electoral behavior: A critical review. *Political Behavior* 1:137–43.

———. 1980. A French political business cycle? In *French Politics and Public Policy,* ed. Philip G. Cerny and Martin A. Schain, 142–58. London and New York: Methuen and St. Martin's.

———. 1983. Political manipulation of the economy: A closer look at political business cycles. *Presidential Studies Quarterly* 13:37–49.

Mosley, Paul. 1978. Images of the "floating voter": Or the "political business cycle" revisited. *Political Studies* 26:375–94.

Mughan, Anthony. 1987. General election forecasting in Britain: A comparison of three models. *Electoral Studies* 6:195–207.

Nordhaus, W. 1975. The political business cycle. *Review of Economic Studies* 42:169–90.

Norpoth, Helmut. 1984. Economics, politics and the cycle of presidential popularity. *Political Behavior* 6:252–73.

———. 1985. The economy and presidential popularity in the United States. Paper presented at the 13th World Congress of the International Political Science Association, July 15–20, Paris.

———. 1987. Guns and butter and government popularity in Britain. *American Political Science Review* 81:949–60.

Norpoth, H., and Yantek, Thomas. 1983. Von Adenauer bis Schmidt: Wirtschaftslage und Kanzlerpopularitat. In *Wahlen und Politisches System, Analysen aus Anlass der Bundestagswahl 1980,* ed. M. Kasse and H.-D. Klingemann, 174–97. Opladen: Westdeutscher Verlag.

Oppenheimer, Bruce I.; Stimson, James A.; and Waterman, Richard W. 1986. Interpreting U.S. congressional elections: The exposure thesis. *Legislative Studies Quarterly* 11:227–47.

Owens, J. R., and Olson, G. C. 1980. Economic fluctuations and congressional elections. *American Journal of Political Science* 24:469–93.

Page, Benjamin, and Jones, Calvin. 1979. Reciprocal effects of policy preferences, party loyalties and the vote. *American Political Science Review* 73:1071–89.

Paldam, Martin. 1981a. A preliminary survey of the theories and findings on vote and popularity functions. *European Journal of Political Research* 7:1–26.

————. 1981b. An essay on the rationality of economic policy: The test-case of the electional cycle. *Public Choice* 37:287–305.

————. 1986. The distribution of election results and the two explanations of the cost of ruling. *European Journal of Political Economy* 2:5–24.

Paldam, Martin, and Schneider, Friedrich. 1980. The macroeconomic aspects of government and opposition popularity in Denmark 1957–78. *National Okonomisk Tidsskrift* 118:149–70.

Parisi, A., and Pasquino, G., eds. 1977. *Continuita e mutamento elettorale in Italia.* Bologna: Societa Editrice il Mulino.

Peffley, Mark. 1984. The voter as juror: Attributing responsibility for economic conditions. *Political Behavior* 6, no. 3: 275–94.

Percheron, Annick, and Jennings, M. Kent. 1981. Political continuities in French families. *Comparative Politics* 13:421–36.

Peretz, Paul. 1981. The effect of economic change on political parties in West Germany. In Hibbs and Fassbender 1981, 101–20.

Pindyck, Robert S., and Rubinfeld, Daniel. 1982. *Econometric Models and Economic Forecasts.* 2d ed. New York: McGraw-Hill.

Pissarides, C. A. 1980. British government popularity and economic performance. *Economic Journal* 90:569–81.

Powell, G. Bingham, Jr. 1983. The science of politics: Cleavages, party identification and accountability in comparative voting behavior. Paper presented at the annual meeting of the American Political Science Association, August–September, Chicago.

————. 1987. Constitutional design and citizen electoral control. Paper presented at the annual meeting of the American Political Science Association, August–September, Washington, D.C.

Putnam, Robert D. 1973. *The Beliefs of Politicians: Ideology, Conflict, and Democracy in Britain and Italy.* New Haven: Yale University Press.

Rattinger, Hans. 1981. Unemployment and the 1976 election in Germany: Some findings at the aggregate and the individual level of analysis. In Hibbs Fassbender 1981, 121–35.

Rivers, Douglas. 1988. Macro-economics and macropolitics: A solution to the Kramer problem. *American Political Science Review,* forthcoming.

Ronning, G., and Schneider, F. 1976. Popularitatsfunktionn—eine empirische Zwei-Lander-Studie. *Jahrbuch für Soialwissenschaft* 27:370–90.

Rosa, Jean-Jacques, and Amson, Daniel. 1976. Conditions économiques et élections: une analyse politico-econometrique (1920–1973). *Revue française de science politique* 26:1101–24.

Rose, Richard. 1982. From simple determinism to interactive models of voting. *Comparative Political Studies* 15:145–69.

Rose, Richard, and Urwin, Derek. 1969. Social cohesion, political parties and strains in regimes. *Comparative Political Studies* 2:7–67.

Rosenstone, S. J.; Hansen, J. M.; and Kinder, D. R. 1983. Measuring personal economic well-being. Report submitted to the Board of Overseers, United States National Election Study and the 1984 National Election Study Planning Committee.

Samuelson, Paul A. 1976. *Economics.* 10th ed. New York: McGraw-Hill.

Sanders, David; Ward, Hugh; and Marsh, David. 1987. Government popularity and the Falklands war: A reassessment. *British Journal of Political Science* 17:281–313.

Sani, Giacomo. 1973. Fattori determinanti delle preferenze partitiche in Italia. *Rivista Italiana de scienza politica* 3:1229–43.

———. 1977. The Italian electorate in the mid-1970s: Beyond tradition? In *Italy at the Polls,* ed. Howard R. Penniman, 81–122. Washington, D.C.: American Enterprise Institute.

———. 1978. La composizione degli elettorati communista e democristiano. In *La politica nell' Italia che Cambia,* ed. A. Martinelle and G. Pasquino. Milan: Feltrinelli.

Santagata, Walter. 1981. Ciclo politico-economice: il case Italiano, 1953–1979. *Stato e mercato* 2:257–99.

———. 1982. On the demand for macroeconomic outcomes and politicians' beliefs: The Italian case. Working paper no. 4. Laboratorio de economia politica. Turin: Universita degli studi di Torino.

Sartori, Giovanni. 1966. European political parties: The case of polarized pluralism. In *Political Parties and Political Development,* ed. Joseph Lapalombara and Myron Weiner, 137–76. Princeton: Princeton University Press.

———. 1976. *Parties and Party Systems: A Framework for Analysis.* Cambridge: Cambridge University Press.

Schlozman, K., and Verba, S. 1979. *Injury to Insult.* Cambridge: Harvard University Press.

Schneider, F. 1985. Public attitudes toward economic conditions and their impact on government behavior. In Eulau and Lewis-Beck 1985, 15–31.

Schneider, F., and Pommerehne, W. W. 1980. Politico-economic interactions in Australia: Some empirical evidence. *Economic Record* 56:113–31.

Sears, David O., and Lau, Richard R. 1983. Inducing apparently self-interested political preferences. *American Journal of Political Science* 27:223–52.

Sigelman, Lee. 1983. Mass political support in Sweden: Retesting a political-economic model. *Scandinavian Political Studies* 6:309–15.

Sigelman, Lee, and Tsai, Y. 1981. A reanalysis of the linkage between personal finances and voting behavior. *American Politics Quarterly* 9:371–99.

Skocpol, Theda, and Finegold, Kenneth. 1982. State capacity and economic intervention in the early New Deal. *Political Science Quarterly* 97:255–78.

Stigler, G. 1973. General economic conditions and national elections. *American Economic Review, Papers and Proceedings* 63:160–67.

Stimson, James A. 1985. Regression in space and time: A statistical essay. *American Journal of Political Science* 29:914–47.

Swank, Duane. 1988. Political economic cycles and U.S. fiscal policies in executive and legislative arenas, 1958–1987. Paper presented at the annual meeting of the Midwest Political Science Association, April 14–16, Chicago.

Tetlock, P. E. 1983. Cognitive style and political ideology. *Journal of Personality and Social Psychology* 45:118–26.

Tobin, James. 1980. Stabilization policy ten years after. *Brookings Papers on Economic Activity* 1:1–82.

Tourangeau, R. 1984. Cognitive science and survey methods. In *Cognitive Aspects of Survey Methodology: Building a Bridge between Disciplines,* ed. T. Jabine, M. Straf, J. Tanur, and R. Tourangeau. Washington, D.C.: National Academy Press.

Tufte, Edward R. 1975. Determinants of the outcomes of midterm congressional elections. *American Political Science Review* 69:812–26.

———. 1978. *Political Control of the Economy.* Princeton: Princeton University Press.

Tyler, T. R.; Rasinski, K. A.; and McGraw, K. M. 1985. The influence of perceived injustice upon support for the president, political authorities and government institutions. *Journal of Applied Social Psychology* 15:700–725.

van der Eijk, C., and Niemoller, B. 1983. Ideology, party identification and rational voting in the Netherlands. Paper presented at the annual meeting of the American Political Science Association. August–September, Chicago.

Wall, Joseph Frazier. 1978. *Iowa: A History.* New York: Norton.

Weatherford, M. Stephen. 1978. Economic conditions and electoral outcomes: Class differences in the political response to recession. *American Journal of Political Science* 22:917–38.

———. 1983. Economic voting and the "symbolic politics" argument: A reinterpretation and synthesis. *American Political Science Review* 77:158–74.

Weiner, Bernard. 1982. The emotional consequences of causal attributions. In *Affect and Cognition,* ed. M. S. Clark and S. T. Fiske, 185–209. Hillsdale, N.J.: Lawrence Erlbaum.

Weiner, Bernard; Frieze, I.; Kukla, A.; Reed, L.; Rest, S.; and Rosenbaum, R. M. 1972. Perceiving the causes of success and failure. In *Attribution: Perceiving the Causes of Social Behavior,* ed. E. E. Jones. Morristown, N.J.: General Learning Press.

Weisberg, Herbert F., and Bowen, Bruce D. 1977. *An Introduction to Survey Research and Data Analysis.* San Francisco: W. H. Freeman.

Whiteley, Paul F. 1986. Macroeconomic performance and government popularity in Britain: The short-run dynamics. *European Journal of Political Research* 14:45–61.

Whiteley, Paul F., ed. 1980. *Models of Political Economy.* London and Beverly Hills: Sage.

Winters, Richard; Johnson, Cathy; Nowosadko, P.; and Rendine, J. 1981. Political behavior and American public policy: The case of the political business cycle. In *Handbook of Political Behavior,* ed. Samuel Long. New York: Plenum.

Witt, Evans. 1983. A model election? *Public Opinion* 5, no. 6 (December/January): 46–49.

Wright, Gavin. 1974. The political economy of New Deal spending: An econometric analysis. *Review of Economics and Statistics* 56:30–39.

Zajonc, R. B. 1980. Feeling and thinking: Preferences need no inferences. *American Psychologist* 35:151–75.

Index